CRASH BOATS OF GORLESTON

Second edition 2011
First published in 2005 by

WOODFIELD PUBLISHING LTD
Bognor Regis, West Sussex, England
www.woodfieldpublishing.co.uk

ISBN 1-903953-84-7

Crash Boats of Gorleston

An illustrated history of No. 24 RAF Air/Sea Rescue Unit, Gorleston-on-Sea, Norfolk

T ONY O VERILL

Woodfield

Dedicated to my father
LAC Overill – MBC on HSLs 108 & 116

and to all the officers, NCOs and crews
who served at 24 A.S.R.U. Gorleston-on-Sea
in war and peace

LAC Overill (with the Author), Great Yarmouth, September 1940.

Contents

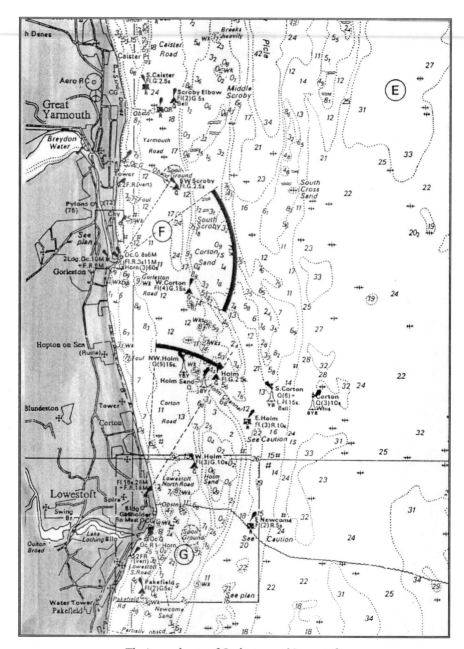

The ins and outs of Gorleston and Lowestoft.

Foreword

This book is dedicated to the efforts of those who, day in and day out, risked their lives to save others, who endured all that the sea could inflict, who faced gunfire with the same courage and stoicism with which they faced the weather, who endured days and nights of cold boredom, searching the wave crests and hollows for that elusive speck which signified a helpless man, or all too often, a lifeless body.

Over the centuries the East Anglian coast has been a graveyard for hundreds of ships, costing thousands of lives, and from these tragedies arose a history of lifesaving unequalled in any other part of the world. At the centre of all this activity was, and still is, the Port of Great Yarmouth and its neighbour Gorleston, the haven of Yarmouth Roadstead inside the Scroby Sands.

This district was not only famous for lifesaving but for the development of lifesaving craft from Breeching's Norfolk and Suffolk; the most famous and enduring principle and design, to the as yet unacknowledged development of fast inflatables by Mr Claude Peacock, a former Gorleston volunteer lifeboatman. On the quayside at Gorleston three lifeboat houses can still be traced from the original five which existed at the beginning of the 20th century. During World War 2, on the banks of the rivers Thurne and Waveney, many high-speed launches (HSLs) and similar rescue craft were built, as well as almost eighty RAF airborne lifeboats.

As navigation, ship and tackle design and strength improved, so the dreadful annual toll of lives diminished – until the 1939-45 war, when many aircraft, as well as ships, became casualties at sea, due to enemy action, mechanical failure or bad weather.

During this period it was fitting that Yarmouth's neighbour Gorleston-on-Sea should continue the local lifesaving traditions by becoming home to Number 24 A.S.R.U. – the top British Air Sea Rescue Unit of the Royal Air Force.

This story has, perforce, to gloss over the hundreds of hours of HSL sea duty, when the cold and the monotony nibbled away at awareness and concentration, and weary bodies protested at the constant movement and inevitable bruising from repeated contact with hard surfaces.

Frequently, the sea was a greater enemy than the Germans, and it is worth remembering that pick-ups were made regardless of whether the man in the sea was a comrade in arms or an enemy who had been shooting at you a few minutes previously.

This tribute book is long overdue, as the sterling efforts of the courageous rescue crews, who carried out their onerous duties with little in the way of reward or recognition, deserve to be chronicled, especially given that today's state medals seem to be awarded without the need for heroic deeds or exemplary services; sadly times change and yesterday's values are not necessarily the same as today's.

Stephen Brewster Daniels

Introduction

The Origins of the Royal Air Force Marine Service

On 1st April 1918 the Royal Flying Corps and the Royal Naval Air Service were joined together into one service and the Royal Air Force was formed. Until that time the Royal Flying Corps had operated only land-based aircraft, whereas the Royal Naval Air Service had operated both land and sea-based types. Because a variety of small boats were needed for flying-boat and seaplane operations, a number of these craft, along with the personnel to operate them, were transferred from the Royal Naval Air Service to become the first members of the RAF Marine Service.

In the 1920s great progress was being made in linking the far-flung British Empire by air and the flying boats of the Royal Air Force played a significant role in developing these air routes. Thus flying boat squadrons became established at several large bases around the coast of the UK, the main ones being Calshot, Cattewater (later to be known as Plymouth Mountbatten) and Felixstowe. With other bases being established abroad, the need to develop the special techniques required for the efficient operating of flying boats, coupled with the gradual emergence of the Royal Air Force as the third service but with its own unique identity, brought in its turn a change of outlook to the 'airmen' manning marine craft.

Little thought was given, at this stage, to the need for specialised rescue craft, for flying boats had an excellent safety record. However, with the formation of the High Speed Flight to compete for the Schneider Trophy there were a few who saw the need for fast craft to be ready in case of an accident, because of the high speed at which these new seaplanes travelled.

Until the late 1920s the Admiralty was responsible for the design and procurement of all Royal Air Force marine craft, so naturally these were adapted RN types. After being given responsibility for procuring their own craft, the Air Ministry continued to place orders with the boatyards traditionally used by the Admiralty, but began to look for new designs suitable for the special roles of RAF Marine Craft.

Many people are aware of the legend of Colonel T.E. Lawrence in connection with his deeds in Arabia in World War One; but what of his later days? Upon his return to England after his Middle East exploits, Lawrence, at first a national hero, became the centre of a heated debate. Feeling that everything was getting out of hand and having no wish to be a public figure, he left the army and sought a personal peace as Aircraftsman Ross in the Royal Air Force in 1922. In 1923 he had to leave the Air Force as the presence in the ranks caused embarrassment to the officers. He quickly enlisted in the Tank Corps at Bovington Camp under another assumed name, that of T.E. Shaw. In 1925 he was allowed to quietly transfer back into the Royal Air Force. After a year's service in India he was posted to the Royal Air Force Marine Base Cattewater (today known as Plymouth Mountbatten) in January 1928. Upon his arrival at the station he became interested in the development of marine craft and this was to last until his retirement in 1935.

Shaw's passion for fast motor cycles was well known, so it was not surprising that he became engrossed in motorboats. He gained experience in his own craft "Biscayne Baby" and was often to be found speeding across Plymouth Sound in all kinds of weather. Because of his experience he was given the task of testing the 37-foot Seaplane Tender built by Scott-Paine to an order placed by the Air Ministry through Flt Lt Beauforte-Greenwood, who backed the British Power Boat Company's claims for the 'hard chine' type of marine craft.

The Marine Service had seen nothing like this to date: it was powered by two 100hp engines and had a speed of 23 knots; it was easy to handle and stood up well to heavy weather. As a result of Shaw's report the Seaplane Tender was ordered in large numbers and Shaw soon found himself working closely on the development of other craft being built at Hythe for the Royal Air Force.

It is thought that he was involved in the development of the first fast Crash Boat, later to be known as a High Speed Launch (HSL). When this type of craft reached the Marine Unit at Calshot in 1936 the airmen/seamen began to ponder upon the possibility that Shaw might be someone a little bit special after all, and not just a chap who was neither one thing nor the other.

Within a regrettably short space of time Lawrence was tragically killed and never lived to see the end product of his efforts. Scott-Paine however, saw all his predictions and efforts brought to fruition. He lived in Greenwich, USA and died there in 1954 after several years of debilitating illness. It is sad to relate that his endeavours for this country were not properly recognised when he died.

While the work of establishing new air routes continued, great international rivalry over the establishment of new speed and endurance records led to rapid development on land, water and especially in the air. These intense endeavours led to the use of new materials, design techniques and engines of greater and greater power. Names like Henry Seagraves, Parry Thomas, Betty Carstairs, Cdr Garfield Wood, Hubert Scott-Paine and Malcolm Campbell – to mention but a few of this intrepid band – became well known to the public at large and their various records, or even attempted records, caught everyone's attention.

A major spur to increase speed in the air was provided by the Schneider Trophy, the contest for which resulted in the building of lighter engines and the introduction of stressed light metal structures.

On water things were rather different... During World War 1 the well known firm of ship and boat builders, John I. Thorneycroft & Son Limited, had produced very fast light coastal craft for the Admiralty. Like flying boats their underwater hull shape was "stepped". These craft remained the fastest attack craft until the late thirties. Craft of this type were still being built by Thorneycroft for various foreign navies in 1939. After the outbreak of war these craft were promptly requisitioned for service with the Royal Navy.

Several firms competed for the first Motor Torpedo Boat contract and a new firm founded by Hubert Scott-Paine at Hythe in 1927 was successful. Named the British Power Boat Company this company had within a few years of starting up, produced a craft for the Royal Air Force which was to have a resounding effect upon future designs. It was the success of this first design for the Royal Air Force which led to the close association between them, until The British Power Boat Company closed in 1945/6.

Having accepted the first High Speed Launch (HSL) in 1936 the Royal Air Force ordered a further sixteen. On 28th February 1939 Air Vice Marshal Sholto Douglas presided over a meeting which placed responsibility for Air Sea Rescue under Coastal Command. The operational use of marine craft was not discussed at the meeting, but it was decided that a further thirteen marine craft were needed and an order was placed for them.

On August 22nd 1940 Air Marshall Sir Arthur Harris chaired a meeting to draft the organisation of the Air Sea Rescue Service because of the concern of the numbers of aircrew lost by drowning in the Channel and the North Sea. It was decided to continue the skeleton service of Coastal Command with boats from the Naval Auxiliary Patrol and the new Royal Air Force rescue launches would be operated under the control of the local Naval Authorities. The Royal Air Force however would retain responsibility of the twelve Westland Lysander aircraft on loan from the Army Co-operation Command and Fighter Command would control all Search and Rescue operations.

There were no further developments until a proper organization call the Directorate of Air Sea Rescue was formed in mid February 1941. The Navy also allocated craft especially for Air Sea Rescue work.

Thus it was that the first purpose-built Air Sea Rescue launch, HSL 100 was commissioned for the Royal Air Force. These types of craft were conceived and designed by Scott-Paine and Fred Cooper and numbered from HSL 100-121 (inclusive) and were in service before 1939.

Gorleston also saw the beginning and the end in the design of Air Sea Rescue Craft. 1940 saw the arrival of HSLs 108 and 116. These had an overall length in round figures of 64 feet and a beam of 14 feet, 3 x 500 horse power converted aero engines, petrol driven, they carried 950 gallons of high octane fuel and ran at a maximum speed of 40 knots plus. The first of the batch had a single skinned hull, but after tests in stormy seas, it was decided that future craft would be built with a double diagonal skin. This proved a very wise decision and those who rode out the many gales in which these craft later went to sea were thankful for it. The first batch were numbered 100 to 121 but were followed by launches known by their crews as "whalebacks", because their superstructure resembled the outline of a whale's back.

Why the change? The 100 class launch, it was considered, could be improved upon as a seagoing craft, in the interest of the crews serving on them. The first of the 100 class craft was built in 1936 as a peacetime ambulance; it was difficult to get men aboard from the sea because the freeboard was rather high. The Whaleback was 63 feet in length or in RAF terms "LOA" (length overall) and had a 16 feet beam in round figures, 3 x 500hp converted aero engines, petrol driven, all three giving a maximum speed of 36 knots. They carried more fuel than the 100 class, 1,200 gallons with all tanks full. The theory behind the engine layout was that, when on call, no launch would cruise – all launches from Gorleston went flat out until reaching the search area, when the two outboard engines would be cut and the centre engine used to do the search, to conserve fuel.

There were second thoughts about that when a hundred miles and more away from home and safety and when parading up and down the enemy coastline searching for men somewhere in a very small dinghy under the noses of more-than-interested onlookers (and quite good gunners some of them!). Sometimes launches returned to base with just a few gallons of petrol in their tanks after more than a day out in the North Sea, searching sometimes in vain. Initially, launches were unarmed and in some quarters even the Germans referred to them as 'ambulances'. There were even a number of cases where German pilots actually led launches to a dinghy, waggling their wings to say goodbye and flying off home.

Of course, not only British aircrews were rescued; many German airmen were also brought ashore. The scheme was proving successful, too successful for Adolf Hitler, who gave the order for launches to be strafed. This brought about the arming of HSLs, mostly with 303 Vickers gas-operated guns or Lewis machine guns and later, to contend with German aircraft cannon shells, launches were equipped with an Oerlikon gun that fired a heavier calibre shell.

Committees in high places were there to overlook Air Sea Rescue in all its forms and information was fed back to them from operational units worldwide. For instance, the circumstances for launches operating out of Dover, where within 20 miles or so they were in Calais harbour, was a different proposition from that of launches operating out of East Anglian bases, where even after 100 miles there was still some distance to go to get into a Dutch harbour – and many 'pick-ups' had to be made close to the enemy-occupied European mainland.

An appeal to the Royal Navy for some of the larger Fairmile craft, able to stay a sea for longer periods, proved out of the question given the alarmingly high rate of replacements required by the Navy for their Motor Gun Boats and Torpedo Boats lost in scraps with the enemy. (Mind you, they always gave a good account of themselves!) So another design of craft for the RAF was called for, and when the first arrived at Calshot for crewing and commissioning, the first motorboat crew men were not impressed and one rather loudly said "It looks like a Hants and Dorset bus!" – something they were accustomed to seeing on the roads outside the camp.

However, that was to change; her specifications were as follows: LOA 68 feet, beam 17 feet, powered by 3 x 500hp converted aero petrol-driven Napier Sealion engines, maximum speed 28 knots. They were able to stay at sea much longer than their predecessors and without the need to carry drums of high octane fuel lashed to their decks.

The men who had crewed the earlier launches agreed that this was without doubt the best seagoing craft the RAF had ever had – an opinion confirmed by the fact that when hostilities ceased, other launch types were rapidly decommissioned and put into store whereas the 'Hants and Dorsets' continued in service – both in our own coastal waters and abroad.

Calshot was the Mecca of the RAF Marine Craft units during its pre-war days.
[Air Ministry]

HSL 100 – here seen in peacetime at Ramsgate.

Acknowledgements

I must say it was furthest from my thoughts to write a book about the Air Sea Rescue Base at Gorleston-on-Sea, but my good friend Stephen Daniels persuaded me to 'have a go' and presented me with a thick dossier of information to sort out. Many people have helped me with photographs and I would like to thank Mr Willimet and Mr Steadman for photographs and information relating to the Gorleston Lifeboat, Mr Grealy, for his information on German Aircraft which crashed off the East Anglian Coast, Mr Ray Allard, for photographs, and information, on the Baker Street Huts, Mr Graham Joule for his photographs and information on the Rescue Floats and RTTLs, and Mr Don Thurston from the Flixton Air Museum. I am also greatly indebted to my good friend Gloria Webb for her patience and indulgence in typing-up my scribbles and correcting my spelling and punctuation, also Sarah Robinson, for doing likewise. And finally I would like to thank all those people whom I have telephoned to cross reference dates and information such as squadron numbers, types of aircraft, boat numbers, etc.

I have not tried to give a day-by-day account, but have instead focussed on important incidents. As one 24 ASRU veteran said to me, "these days I like to read photographs".

I have referred to other books, namely: *Battle of the Narrow Seas* by Peter Scott, *Rescue From The Skies* by Stephen Daniels, *Air Sea Rescue in World War II* by Alan Rowe and *Battle of The East Coast 1939-1945* by Julian Foynes.

Thanks must also go to my good friend Charles Meacock for his information and clarification of facts concerning 24 ASRU Gorleston on Sea and also to the members of the East Anglian Branch of the Air Sea Rescue/Marine Craft Sections Club for their help, especially concerning the years 1945 to 1961, and finally to the Honorary Secretary of the Anglian Branch ARS/MCS Club, Tony Campling, for the many hours he spent typing the manuscript into his computer and for his invaluable help.

HSL 108 was based at Ramsgate. The crew was as follows: F/O Clarkson, Flt.Sgt Broster, LACs T. Dawson. F. Ingleton. H. Jeffery B. Jones, B. Chackfield and B. Brooks.

HSL 108 pictured whilst cruising of Ramsgate [R. Brooks]

1. Long Ago and Far Away

For holidaymakers on the East Coast, the long hot summer days of 1939 were, unknowingly, the last days of peace. Most of the small towns and villages relied on the holiday and fishing industries, and although hours were long and wages small, life was peaceful and contented. However, this idyll was coming to an end and the storm clouds of war were gathering over the continent of Europe.

On 1st September 1939 the German nation declared war on Poland and the British waited and held their breath... but on 3rd September 1939 they turned on their radio sets to hear Prime Minister Neville Chamberlain declare war on Germany.

After many humiliating defeats and retreats on the continent of Europe, which culminated in the evacuation of the remnants of the British Expeditionary Force from Dunkirk, Europe fell under the heel of the Nazi jackboot. Thus, during the first week of June 1940 the East Coast ports of Harwich, Felixstowe, Lowestoft and Great Yarmouth became, thanks to geography, "on Hitler's back doorstep".

On 2nd June children from these areas were evacuated inland to designated 'safe' areas, and this was the situation when 24 ASRU at Gorleston was commissioned in early 1940.

Gorleston-on-Sea was, at the time, a small fishing town, but in 1940 it was decided by the Air Ministry to set up a small satellite base to RAF Felixstowe for Air Sea Rescue operations and consequently two wooden huts (later increased to four) were built on net-drying land at the bottom of Baker Street. Primarily these were not living accommodation, but crew-ready rooms (temporary accommodation with cooking facilities for 2/3 days) the Officer Commanding, administration and maintenance all being based at Felixstowe, which was the only permanent ASR base on the East Coast in 1939/40, where the early rescue craft based there doubled with crash boats and standby boats for flying boat take-offs and landings.

Unfortunately the marine craft record book for No 24 ASRU Gorleston (Air 29/443) does not begin until 1943. The Admiralty "Red List" (Air/208) however tells us that Gorleston had two permanent boats from January

1941 – HSL108 and HSL116, HSL112 (Felixstowe) being a reserve craft serving both bases.

One notable rescue took place on 19th June 1940, involving boats from Felixstowe and the Gorleston Lifeboat *Louis Stephens* – that of a Wellington, O-Orange, serial no N3200. This rescue was to have a dramatic effect on subsequent events later in the war.

On the night of 19th June 1940 Flight Lt Pickard took off in Wellington O-Orange from RAF Newmarket. His crew consisted of Sgt Broadly, Pilot Officer Thomas and Sergeants Mills, Hanigan and Harniman. Over the target in the Rhur Valley the Wellington was hit by AA fire in the port engine. The aircraft was seriously damaged but despite the loss of power Flt Lt Pickard got the aircraft back to the Dutch Coast and out over the North Sea, but it became obvious that he would have to ditch. He managed to get the aircraft onto the water and his crew into the dinghy. The aircraft had come down some 70 miles off the Norfolk/Suffolk coastline and was surrounded by minefields. HSL108 searched the area for four hours but returned to Felixstowe mid-morning on the 20th June, there having been no sign of a dinghy.

Len Ambler, coxswain of HSL112, another Felixstowe boat, was put on standby and shortly afterwards was ordered out. Once out into the North Sea the launch maintained its course and speed despite the increasing seas. After some considerable time a Wellington aircraft (piloted by P/O Lynes of 99 Squadron) circled the launch firing off red Very lights and then setting off out to sea again. Len Ambler followed it. The seas were worsening and despite a careful lookout there was no sign of the dinghy. Suddenly a flash of yellow was seen on the crest of a wave before it dipped into a trough, but it was enough to give HSL112 a fix, and soon Pickard and his crew, who had been in the dinghy for 15 hours, were picked up, 75 miles due east of Southwold.

As previously stated, this rescue had dramatic consequences, because Flt Lt Pickard went on to star as the pilot of Wellington 'F' Freddie in the wartime propaganda film *Target for Tonight* and later (as Group Captain) led the famous Amiens jail raid, in which the walls of the jail were breached, allowing dozens of French resistance workers to escape.

Tragically, Pickard ('Pick') and his navigator Broadley were killed when their Mosquito aircraft was shot down over the target after he had success-fully led and carried out the raid.

The crew of HSL 108 at Felixstowe. Left to right. Back row. F. Ingleton, not known, L. Taylor (with the cat) B. Chacksfield. Middle row First two names unknown. H. Jeffery. W. Guilfoyle and G. Dunn [Photo F. Ingleton]

*HSL 116 in trials off Felixstowe [**Air Ministry**]*

2. Trials and Tribulations

Not all rescues involved aircrew personnel; some involved the rescue craft themselves, as was the case on 11th May 1941...

HSL 116 was returning to base when the skipper decided to attempt a short-cut, crossing between the Barber Sands and the North Caister Shoal. This was strongly advised against by one of the HSL's crew, LAC Overill, who had fished these waters before the war, but his advice was ignored

At approximately 4.12 am the launch went aground. The Great Yarmouth Coastguard telephoned the Naval Base that the lifeboat was going out to assist an RAF launch that had gone aground. The *Louise Stephens* was launched at 4.45 am, with a stiff north-east breeze blowing and a moderate sea running. The position originally given to the lifeboat crew was the North Scroby shoal, but after searching for some time, they learned at 5.45am that the RAF launch was, in fact, aground on the Caister shoal. The lifeboat went alongside the launch and on discovering that she had lost her propellers proceeded to tow her into port – returning to station at 8.55am. The Official Lifeboat Station Report reads as follows:

> At 4.12 am the coxswain (lifeboat) received a telephone message from the coastguard that the Naval base requests the service of the lifeboat to HSL 116 aground on North Scroby sands. The lifeboat, the "Louise Stephens" was launched at 4.45 am, the position given, North Scroby was searched to no avail. Another wireless message was received at 5.40 am to say that the vessel was aground near the North Caister buoy. On its approach the vessel HSL 116 was becoming afloat on the high tide. The lifeboat went alongside and asked the officer if he required assistance, the officer replied that his propellers had gone and that he needed to be towed back to base. The coxswain C. Johnson took the rope and HSL116 was towed back to Baker Street, Gorleston.

Not all launches that arrived at 24 ASRU were intended visits. On one occasion in February 1941 HSL142 left Grimsby en-route to Felixstowe. The story is told by W/Off Bullock:

> FEBUARY 8th 1941 : Left Grimsby for Dover in HSL 142, intending to reach Felixstowe and stay overnight then proceed to Dover on the next day.
> Whilst cruising at about 30 knots in vicinity of the "Burnham" buoy about 15 miles north east of Cromer, a mine exploded off the starboard quarter and affected the launch to the extent that speed had to be reduced considerably because of the severe vibration and the launch making water. An engineer

suffered severe bruising; I was at the wheel and was thrown across the wheelhouse but escaped injury apart from slight bruising.

We proceeded to Air Sea Rescue unit Gorleston at slow speed, with a Spitfire escort, and was directed by Coastal Command to proceed to Brooke's Boat Yard Oulton Broad on the following day.

We spent three weeks at Brooke's Yard where it was found that the engines had been forced out of alignment, propellers and shafts required replacing and fairly extensive hull damage to be repaired. Crew members were accommodated in private houses in the town whilst repairs were carried out.[1]

I feel that we were fortunate to be travelling at a fairly high speed, otherwise we could have felt the full force of the explosion.

*HSL 116. Author's father in white sweater on extreme right [**Air Ministry**].*

---

[1] It is probable that a German Pilot in a Heinkel 111 Minelayer had spotted the "Burnham" buoy and parachuted the mine where he assumed the channel to be. This route was used extensively used by the inshore convoys, in fact quite close to the area known as "E Boat Alley".

*The original wooden accommodation block No 24 ASRU at Baker Street Gorleston, built in 1940 – Photographed June 1962 [**R.Allard**]*

*No 2 Hut Baker Street Gorleston at No 24 ASRU. Built 1940's when Air Sea Rescue was expanding [**R.Allard**]*

HSL 142 moored alongside HMS Midge, the Royal Naval establishment
after a close encounter with a German mine

East Coast Lifeboats played a very important role in rescues off the Eastern seaboard.
They were always ready to help if the RAF and Navy wanted their assistance.
[Williment Collection]

The Gorleston Lifeboat – The "Louis Stephens" **[Williment Collection]**

3. The 108 Incident

Early in 1941, HSL108, which had been in service since 1938, sailed from Felixstowe for a refit at the Brooke-Marine yard at Lowestoft; during this refit a nest of rats was discovered in the chain locker (an omen, perhaps?). On completion of the refit she was to be based at Baker Street in Gorleston-on-Sea. The crewmembers were to be billeted in civilian 'digs' – a real perk after barrack life. One of these boarding houses was run by a Mrs Florence Styles on Lovewell Road. For one of the crew, LAC Overill, it was to work out even better, as he lived only a couple of miles down the road and, with the aid of a bicycle, would be able to commute between home and the boat.

Although '108' had just undergone a refit she was minus her fresh water tank and, whilst en-route from Lowestoft to Gorleston, hit a partially-submerged railway sleeper, which broke off her Chernikeef log. The following narrative is by R Dagett, MBC, HSL 108.

*

On July 1st 1941 at approximately 1400 hours it was reported that a Blenheim Mk.IV, No.V6288 of 139 Squadron at Horsham St Faiths, had been damaged in a raid and was going to ditch in the North Sea, northwest of Terschelling Island. The launch cleared the harbour bar at 1600 hours; the crew numbered just seven:

Skipper	F/O Jackman
Coxswain	Sgt Hales
Engineer	Raybould
W.Op	Guilfoyle
MBC	P. Drayson, A. Overill, R. Daggert

Thus HSL108 was minus a wireless mechanic and a second engineer.

There was an interesting rumour, never substantiated, that F/O Jackman, an ex-Merchant Navy man from the 1st World War, was of Jewish decent, but as a precaution against possible capture by the Germans had changed his name by leaving the final "n" off his surname, thus anglicising it.

A course had been taken East-North-East for some hours when the crew sighted what they thought was a yellow dinghy, but it turned out to be a Dutch navigational buoy.

In the meantime the Blenheim had been shot down by a Messerschmitt 109F of 1/JG.52 from Leeuwarden in Holland and the three-man crew had taken to their dinghy. A Heinkel 59 floatplane was despatched and picked up the Blenheim crew, taking them to the German Air-Sea Rescue base at Schellingwoude, north of Amsterdam.

After '108' left the navigational buoy to begin the search, two aircraft were seen coming in low and from the west. The crew thought they were RAF aircraft assisting in the search, but it was soon clear that they were German Arado 196 floatplanes. After one run over the launch, they returned and opened fire. The boat was soon riddled with machine gun bullets and a fire started in the engine room. The fire extinguishers were operated and this brought the engines to a standstill. It was obvious that the launch was a sitting duck, so a white flag was hoisted (actually a seaman's white sweater). After a cease-fire, during which the Arado's circled the launch, one eventually alighted on the water. The other continued to circle and cover his comrade.

The coxswain, Sgt Hales, had been slightly injured, but the wireless operator, LAC Guilfoyle, although behind flak matting, had been shot through the chest and had collapsed in his cabin. One of the crew, Peter Drayson, in response to a signal from the German aircraft on the water, paddled the boat's "pram dinghy" towards the Arado. The dinghy had been damaged in the attack and sank on arrival. The aircraft crew pulled Drayson aboard and took off in the direction of the Dutch coast.

After the Arados had left, LAC Overill went over the side with wooden plugs to fill in some of the bullet holes, as by this time the launch was taking water fairly rapidly. Water in the engine room hampered the efforts of Engineer Raybould and all attempts to get even one of the engines going were aborted.

The radio operator, LAC Guilfoyle, was obviously in a bad way, but even so he volunteered to be lifted into the radio cabin to send out an SOS, but he was clearly too weak for this. He asked for water, but there was none on board, so he was given the juice from a tin of fruit and also a morphine injection to relieve his pain. He later came round from this, but there was no more morphine so he was given chloroform instead to deaden the pain. Sadly, he died shortly afterwards. His body was wrapped in a blanket and laid on the starboard side of the deck against the wheelhouse.

By dawn the launch was very low in the water and shortly afterwards the two Arados, this time accompanied by a Heinkel 59, returned. The Arados circled the launch whilst the Heinkel alighted onto the water and taxied up to the launch. The Germans launched a rubber dinghy and started to take the crew back to the aircraft one by one. This was a slow process and with the risk of a surprise attack by allied aircraft they hurried up this operation by ripping off the rear engine cover hatch as an extra means of evacuating the crew of the launch to the Heinkel. Once on board they were given chocolate and told those immortal words ... "For you the war is over."

The Heinkel 59 landed at the German Air-Sea-Rescue base at Schelling-woude north of Amsterdam where they were met by a deputation of senior Luftwaffe Officers, including the Commandant, Dr Possel and, of course, the inevitable propaganda cameramen. They were all given a medical check-up and then transferred to Amsterdam by boat, where they spent several days being interrogated by both Gestapo and Luftwaffe Officers. They were then taken to Dulag-Luft at Frankfurt-Am-Main.

Here they were separated from Skipper Jackman and were transferred to Stalag IX. When the new Luftwaffe camps were completed, the crew was transferred to one of these (Stalag-Luft III).

By a curious twist, the fate of HSL108 was not yet sealed. The launch was no longer seaworthy. Two Vorpostenboats (armed trawlers) VP1108 and VP806 were sent to the area with an order from Luftwaffe Command to sink the HSL. This was disputed by C.I.C. Security North Sea (Kriegsmarine) who wanted to salvage the launch and use it for Naval control for the movement of traffic in the Port of Cuxhaven, and for this reason the launch was saved.

When the HSL was sighted she was drifting into a minefield. Two dinghies were launched from the Vorpostenboats to go aboard. When the boat crews boarded 108, it was deserted apart from the dead W/Op Guilfoyle. After searching the launch and securing the many bullet holes in the hull to maintain buoyancy, Guilfoyle was given a "burial at sea".

The launch was lashed to the side of VP 1108 and taken to Lock No.3 at Wilhemshaven. The salvage of the launch was not simple and not without danger. It is therefore understandable that HSL108 was already promised to Bafehlshaber-Der-Sicherung (BSN) by Gruppe Nord, but after an inter-service wrangle it was handed over to Luftwaffe Command of ships and boats (Nord) at Kiel, the interests of the Kriegsmarine having to take second place to those of the Luftwaffe.

HSL108 was pressed into duty by the Luftwaffe and used for picking up survivors from the German "lobster pot" survival buoys along the Dutch

Coast between Wilhelmshaven and Flushing (now Vissingen). It is remarkable also that during the following months of the war, many aircrew, both Bomber and Fighter command, reported sightings of an RAF Air-Sea Rescue launch operating just off the Dutch Coast. Could this have been HSL108?

Back at Gorleston, due to the limitations of communications in those days, nobody knew for sure what had happened to "108". Had she had been captured by E-boats? Sunk by aircraft? Defected to the Germans? All kinds of rumour were rife, to such and extent that it was forbidden to talk about the incident under sufferance of being placed on a charge. At a higher echelon it was suggested that skipper Jackman had violated radio silence and that possibly the code books had been captured. As the author's father was one of the crew, it can be stated without doubt that none of these things happened. Radio silence was not broken and the code books were correctly disposed of (over the side in a weighted sack). The capture of HSL108 was due to a series of unfortunate circumstances and lack of communication.

1941 was not a good year for the ports or the citizens of Great Yarmouth and Gorleston. Over 7,000 incendiary bombs and 800 high explosive bombs were dropped by the Luftwaffe and killed over 100 civilian, military and naval personnel. The most severe raid was on 8th April 1941, when 4,000 incendiary bombs were dropped. From the Market Place to the South Quay 65 major fires and 200 smaller ones were dealt with by fire brigades from as far afield as Norwich and Cromer. Many well-known shops (including Marks and Spencer & Boots the Chemist) were destroyed, 17 people were killed and 68 injured on that night alone.

One Dornier Do17 was hit by anti-aircraft fire from the Bofors gun battery on the North Pier (Harbour's Mouth). The aircraft ditched and the ASR unit dispatched a launch to pick up survivors. One of the crew managed to swim ashore and was captured by the very gun battery that shot him down. The rest were picked up by the 24 ASRU launch and brought ashore. (The author still has a Nazi tie pin given to his father in gratitude for saving his life.)

Thus 1941 came to a close, with 24 ASRU having one boat, HSL116, with a second, HSL112, commuting between Felixstowe and Gorleston.

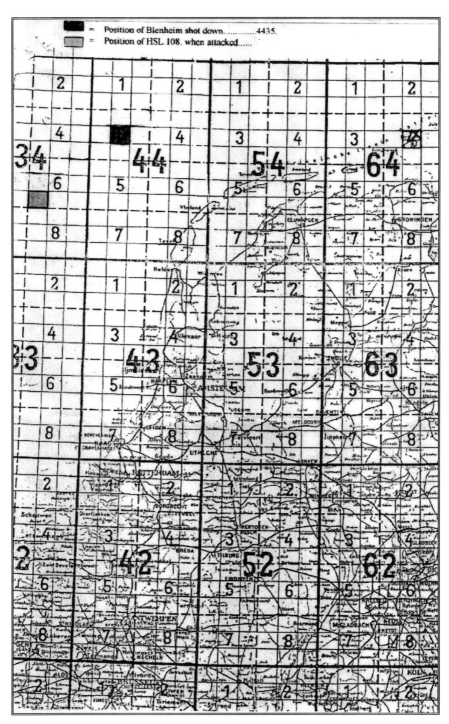

*Part of a German chart depicting the seas off Holland
and indicating where the Capture of HSL 108 was achieved.*

HSL108 tied up alongside the German Coastal Trawler (Vorpostenboot) "VP 1108"
[Photo Roberts]

*HSL 108 in lock No 3 Whilmshaven. Note Luftwaffe Officer and flak damage to and below forward gun turret [**Photo Bundesarghives**]*

*This picture of the crew of HSL 108 was taken at the German ASR base at Schellingwoode. From left to right are- Sgt Hales (slightly wounded) AC Daggett, LAC Overill, LAC Raybould, (the three MBC's are wearing their MaeWests) and Flying Officer Jackman (Skipper) [**Photo RNAF**]*

HSL 108 at Whilmshaven with crosses marking where the German bullets entered and it is likely that the one aft of the gun turret, was the one that killed LAC Guilfoyle when shot from above bearing in mind the angle **Photo Bundesarghives**

*The crew of HSL 108 immediately after being picked up by a Heinkel 59 floatplane., Left to right :- A German Airman, Sgt .Hales, a German Airman. LAC Overill, F/O Jackman, LAC Daggett, LAC Raybould, the German Pilots of the Heinkel 59 Serial marking NE-UY. The names of the German Aircrew are UFFz W.Strauss, FWR Gerster, Lt W.Ehrardt and FWK Logemann. Two German fitters are posed close to the aircraft. [**Photo RNAF**]*

The Heinkel 59, a German Air Sea Rescue Floatplane at Schellingwoode Holland, the photograph was taken by the Dutch Resistance in 1941.
[Photo RNAF]

4. From Depression to Success

Although '108' was captured on 1st July 1941, the unit was to have a success a few days later. On the night of 30th June, four Handley-Page Hampdens from No.49 Squadron took off from Scampton airfield in Lincolnshire to bomb Düsseldorf. Three of the bombers retuned but Hampden X3134 ditched south of Texel Island. The crew survived for nine days in their dinghy on thirty-six Horlicks tablets, half a pint of fresh water and one bar of chocolate. They vainly tried to signal ships and passing aircraft with a mirror, but without success, and had finally resigned themselves to death when they were spotted by HSL 112, some 60 miles off the Dutch port of Ijmuiden. They were weak and exhausted but brought safely back to base.

Of course, not all pick-ups were of British personnel. It must be remembered that at this time the town of Great Yarmouth, and in particular the port and harbour were being continually bombed. The Luftwaffe used the Caister Water Tower as a landmark and then turned south for a direct run over the river Yare. Not all their aircraft managed to complete this manoeuvre unscathed and on 7th March 1941, Dornier 17, Werk No.3391 was shot down by Bofors guns defending the harbour and crashed off Gorleston beach. Two of the aircrew were rescued by a Gorleston ASR launch (HSL 108 or 116). One crewman died and the other swam ashore to be captured by personnel from the coastal artillery battery. During 1941 No24 ASRU must have been very busy, as the author's records show that between January and September of that year no less than 14 enemy aircraft were shot down off the coast of Great Yarmouth.

One interesting incident that occurred early on in the year indicated that chivalry had not entirely gone from modern warfare. One HSL, far out at sea on a crash call, suddenly spotted a Heinkel bomber flying towards them, but it flew low over the water and passed the launch. A white scarf or towel was waving from one of the gun positions and it flew around and around the boat. It made off in a north east direction for some twelve miles and circled again until the launch caught up. There they found the crew of a German bomber, weak and exhausted. They were taken aboard the boat and returned to base. The Heinkel then once more circled the boat, dipping its wings in salute, then it was gone...

5. The Build-Up

1941 ended with a replacement for HSL108 – namely HSL130 – com ing up from Dover. This was a new, improved 'whaleback' launch. On 13th January 1942 she was joined by HSL124 and HSL132, the new whalebacks taking over from the early 100 Series (HSL116 going for a refit at Brooke Marine, Lowestoft in late 1941).

No.24 ASRU was starting to expand. The Cliff Hotel, high above the harbour mouth was taken as the new permanent home for ASR crews (previously they were housed in private billets) and the duty crews in wooden barrack huts in Baker Street.

The following narrative is by Charles Meacock, one of the crew of HSL130, about his arrival at No.24 ASRU:

> "I came up with two other lads, Freddie Sandon and Thomas Ladd. The first thing we saw was a mast with the RAF Ensign flying, this was just above the harbour wall, and it must have been low tide. We were taken up to the Cliff Hotel where an NCO told us to sort ourselves out and then report downstairs.
>
> The hotel had not been used since the outbreak of war, judging by the dirt and rubbish that had piled up. We were told that it was our job to get the place habitable for future crews to take up residence. Our first task was to de-rust the fires and boilers and get the heating and the hot water system working. Once we had hot water it was down to scrubbing brushes, soap and good old-fashioned 'elbow grease' to get the rooms clean, tidy and ready for occupation. The toilets and baths were in a greasy state, but with plenty of Vim we got them back to where they should have been. Finally the day came in February when the RAF crews occupied the Cliff Hotel – NCOs on the upper floor and other ranks on the ground floor. My room on the first floor was situated where we could see the entrance to the River Yare and those heavy North Sea rollers beating on the beach.
>
> We only got a fleeting glimpse of the Launches – HSL 116 was having a refit at Brooke Marine and the crews of HSLs 130, 132 and 124 were taking up residence. We 'erks' were assigned the menial tasks of cooking, stoking the boilers and spud-peeling. On one occasion I wandered down to look at the Launches. The tide was about half way above the timbers that formed the capping of the harbour wall when HSL130 headed downriver with HSL124 astern, which indicated that HSL130 was duty launch, HSL124 was on standby and HSL 132 was on stand- down. The implication of this was that the duty crews remained in close proximity to the duty launch, either at sea or in the crew room.

The standby crewmen were allowed to visit the local canteen or cinema, where in the event of a call-out a message would be flashed up onto the screen for them to return to base. The cinema was only 200 yards up the road so they could return quickly. For the others, the call-out signal was a very noisy klaxon, which could be heard all over Gorleston. The furthest the stand-down crews were allowed to go was Great Yarmouth.

Invariably a call-out would be a two-launch task, and under these conditions competition between crews was fierce. It was similar to a "fighter scramble". Once the phones rang and information was received, all launches with engines running were ready to receive their crews, and we would, in minutes be heading under way towards the mouth of the River Yare. It would then develop into a race as to who could cross the Harbour Bar first. Skippers laying off courses, the initial one given to the first Coxswain who would be at the helm, setting the compass and controlling the engine revs and steerage. Like fighter pilots in the air, the repartee between launches was brisk until the crews would be told to shut up and get on with the job in hand.

Thus it was that the duty launches would go to sea.

It was under these circumstances that from shovelling coal into the Cliff Hotel boilers and spud bashing, I managed a quick look around HSL 130. I felt a tap on my shoulder and looking around saw Flt/Sgt Leslie Flower, who asked what I was doing here. I explained and was given a quick tour of the launch. He asked what I was doing at present and I told him "Spud bashing and feeding the Cliff Hotel's boilers" – a point which he seemed to take on board, for within a few days Freddie, Thomas and myself were assigned to HSL130. My first task was to polish the brass on the control panel and tidy the forecastle, which was the crews quarters (even though they lived ashore). It was quite an experience to be in the engine room when all three engines burst into life. I seized every opportunity to be aboard and this involved me doing "anchor watch" – to let out the mooring lines when the tide fell, or to take them in when it rose. Other times I spent fishing with a hand-line, which often resulted in a "fry-up" of small codling or whiting.

My first experience of a "klaxon call-out" was something of an accident. I was in the forecastle toilet and once we were under way I presented myself at the wheelhouse, where everybody was very busy and I was told to "go aft to the sick bay". Then one of the deckhands suggested I should get into the aft turret, not a place for the claustrophobic or to be in anything but a flat-calm sea. This call-out was for us to go and despatch a barrage balloon which had come adrift and landed, fully inflated, in the sea lanes. Our coxswain got within range and shut engines and the order was given to open fire. I have never found out what law comes into force when firing guns at sea, but there was this massive balloon and all shots seem to miss. I'm sure that balloon was taking the Mickey and I suppose it deserved to survive, but Flt/Sgt Flower ordered .303 Enfields brought up and some well-aimed rounds finally saw the balloon deflate and sink beneath the waves. We returned to base and the lads went ashore.

I was left to complete my task of tidying up, convinced that being in a gun turret on a launch at sea wasn't exactly a plum job.

With much bad weather, little bombing activity took place and convoys through "E-boat" Alley in the North Sea were minimal, albeit late one evening a single boat call out was requested in the direction of Cromer and search for crew down in that area. It happened that HSL 130 was duty launch, but whilst the Yare itself was comparatively quiet, however, once we had reached the entrance to the sea, it got blustery and very rough, one minute the bow was pointing to heaven as if praying to return and the next minute it was plunging towards Davy Jones's locker, shuddering at the thought of going further and to add to the pleasant thoughts that surround this experience the Wireless operator reported to the Skipper and the first Coxswain that a gale warning had been issued and that he had intercepted an Admiralty message for all coastal craft to return to base.

However we were no ordinary navy, and there was a crew out there that had to be saved, so we bashed on. I had never had the experience before or for that matter since, and I have been out into some gales in my time. For start no one told me I was joining the submarine service, all the hatches had to be battened down thank god, I fully expected to see a shoal of fish passing the portholes, quite often there was a terrific whirring noise created by the engines as the propellers presented themselves to God's heaven devoid of seawater to "beat up" upside down? I am sure of it, me being a land lubber with little seafaring experience succumbed to the inevitable; "The bucket is in the corner!" yelled a helpful voice, from this point on, upside down – down side up, I wasn't caring. I didn't pass out, but perhaps it would have been better for me if I had done so. I remember Jock Bryce emerging from his radio cabin and reporting that we were to return to base (RTB), he asked me if I was alright to which I replied "not too bad", and understatement if ever there was one. Suddenly everything became calm and quiet, we were back in the Yare, and shortly afterwards moored up with the engines cut, a welcomed silence descended on the base. Thank God, for Leslie Flower, who had got us back safely.

"Jock" Laurence Bryce came to see if I wanted help to get ashore, but I managed it under my own steam, never the less Laurence stood by and pleased to say that he did, for once I got my feet onto dry land it rocked as if in a minor earthquake, the buildings moved and altogether it was not a nice sensation, Laurence kindly saw me to my bunk (bed) at the Cliff Hotel where before I went to sleep I wondered what I could re-muster to avoid such punishment? The next morning herald a new day and I dismissed the re-mustering idea as a cowardly thing to do, and by the time I had done the polishing and tidying up of the "old darling", everything in her had taken a bashing, she looked as though she had been in a storm! The thoughts of being anything other than a MBC (motor boat crewman) had gone.

The information that filtered down to the crew that day was that Coxswain Blogg of the Cromer Lifeboat had picked up the aircrew and they were ashore and in bed whilst we were being buffeted by the North Sea. Someone said, "C'est la Guerre!"

The Cliff Hotel was a good listening post for "things" going on at sea, like a convoy proceeding up the channel or some ding dong between "E" boats and our own Navy Motor Gun Boats which moored opposite to us in the Yare. After such a "thunderstorm" one night, the base received a two launch call out around daybreak to a position somewhere in the shipping lanes off Felixstowe.

As stated earlier when two launches were involved, the rivalry was keen and HSL 132 Coxswain Flt/Sgt Brown lay ahead of us in the Yare, so after 6 claps of thunder all engines on the two launches were ready and we were riding on heavy lines awaiting the two skippers to arrive. I think there was nothing in the sprint from the base by the skippers to the launches, it was the fact that the HSL 132 lay ahead of us that she left the Yare first, some three hundred yards ahead of us, the most important man on the launch was the 1st Coxswain, and during training on the courses, one was given the details about fuel consumption, cruising speeds and maximum revs advisable and so on, but all of that went out of the porthole during a "call-out"

At this stage HSL 132 proceeded ahead of us, a deckhand or perhaps a fitter appeared on the stern dangling a tow rope, suffice it to say with Leslie at the helm and three well tuned engines, we arrived on the scene a little before HSL 132, but being gentlemen we left the tow rope in the locker. One can imagine the crew of 132 with their heads down discussing how we did it and what they could do about it? However the scene set before us was that of a minesweeper, low down in the water, not too low however, with her port deck lined with "ginger haired" sailors dressed in white uniforms. We drew alongside and moored up and after some interchange of information between the Skipper and a Naval Officer, we embarked 13 of these sailor lads, let go our moorings and headed full speed for Felixstowe where a radio message "in code" assured that ambulances would be awaiting our arrival. Once they were aboard, the white uniforms became the normal sailor's uniformed covered in "flour". I think it was plain flour, rather that self raising!

It was only several days later after we had heard that they had been struck by a mine, that my mind sent out signals saying their hair must have been singed by the explosion, until then I was beginning to think that to be ginger and be at sea was unlucky, one of my own pals on the base was ginger!!, how a mine sweeper managed to get herself blown up with a mine was a mystery until it was established that Jerry was using something new and to be known as the magnetic mine.

We made Felixstowe harbour, in record time where a number of ambulances were waiting and we discharged our group of sailors then headed back to Gorleston, HSL 132 ferried the remainder of those sailors who were also burnt to Felixstowe and later returned to Gorleston where we both refuelled and stood ready for the next call. This was around April/May time and HSL 130 was due for a repaint, anti fouling and general refit, so we proceeded to Lowestoft and I recall going through a lock and us being slipped in Brooke's yard. It was a scratch crew that ferried her there as this was an opportunity for leave for the crew and I was left as "boat watch" whilst the others returned to Gorleston.

On the detail of this, my memory has faded, how long she was there, I cannot remember, but it was not long. I recall the batteries being collected to return to Gorleston for recharging. She was back at Gorleston in May during which time Flt/Sgt Leslie Flower gave of his time to give me instruction in the tasks expected of a MBC, but went further and explained the charts used for navigation and how to establish a course and measure distances on a chart, and advised me to buy a very useful book "the Yacht Master's Guide and Coaster" companion which I studied and carried with me throughout the war, and which has pride of place on one of my bookshelves.

Here is a convenient point to tell you something about the men, the qualities, qualifications and the calibre of those who manned these craft, "all volunteers" The launches based at Gorleston in January 1942 were HSLs 124, 130 and 132 all called "Whalebacks". The crews consisted of:

- The Master or Skipper [as the men called him] and to which he would respond
- 1st Coxswain
- 2nd Coxswain
- thee deckhands, known as MBCs (motor boat crew)
- two Wireless Operators
- two Fitters/Marine
- one Medical Orderly.

The qualifications to become a master/skipper varied, either it was someone who had started as an MBC (motor boat crewman) and had taken courses to qualify as a 1st Class Coxswain, recommended for a commission, taken a further course and passed the course, when he would be commissioned. However the opportunity for such a man did not come at the beginning of the war, only with the rapid expansion of the Air Sea Rescue and Marine Craft Section brought this about. Men were recruited from the Royal Navy from those who held a commission or from the Merchant Navy from those holding a Mate's Ticket or who were a Master Mariner.

1st Class Coxswains would have undergone three specialist training courses involving practice and theory in all cases, first as an MBC, secondly as a second class Coxswain and finally a first class Coxswain's course. All were intensive courses each subsequent one going into a subject already dealt with but to a much greater degree. The second class Coxswain's course would deal with Navigation at a depth sufficient that should any one of them be left to get the launch home, however hazardous the conditions and the waters to be navigated, he is capable of coping with it. This did happen on a number of occasions. Each member of the crew had an expertise second to none, as was to be proven on so many occasions.

At all times, a crew was a rather special group of men, no matter what your trade was, if help was needed you did not have to ask a second time. Medical orderlies have helped to get an engine lifted out of the engine room. I have seen every member of the crew at some time or other on the helm. Getting a poor injured soul out of the sea, lads would go down the scramble nets to get them aboard, and get soaking wet it might be a coxswain, deckhand, nursing orderly, officer whoever was handy. To this day if you are a member of one of these crews you are known as a "webfoot".

All in their turn have cooked meals, made the tea and done sundry other jobs, we have good cause to be proud of our Royal Navy down the years of history, well here is another Navy the Royal Air Force Navy, a grand bunch of men, lads who were responsible for saving of the order of 14,000 lives, and that made many Mothers, Fathers, Brothers and Sisters and sweethearts very, very happy. Anyone at sea needing help got it, ASR was not exclusive for RAF aircrews.

The Master [or skipper to the lads] was a Commissioned Officer holding the rank of Pilot or Flying Officer or that of Flight Lieutenant; very few of them were able to fly aircraft, but waterborne they were in their element. Informality afloat was one thing but ashore the Kings Commission and KKRs (Kings Rules and Regulations) were respected and observed by all.

Life was quiet for a while and routine until one day a Dornier decided to fly at mast height down the Yare, being near the entrance to the Yare where he made his approach from, gave us no time to man the guns, but some of the lads at the Yarmouth end of the river sounded as though they got a crack at him. As no report filtered down of a hit or downed Jerry, we presume he got home safely; he was low enough to see his face. Again another peaceful spell disturbed only by members of the Yarmouth constabulary. I was aboard HSL 130 doing my chores, when I was approached by two plain clothed officers asking me to row them across the river to the Naval base, which of course I could not do without permission of an Officer or the coxswain of the launch. It transpired that they were undertaking an investigation into an illicit Rum trade going on in Yarmouth. The coxswain came out to confirm my story and I was told to row them across to the Motor Gun Boat base, which I did, later the Naval lads returned them to our side. It seemed that the Navy boys had nothing to do with the Rum trade so the report said. At the end of May, beginning of June I, and the other two lads who arrived for the opening of the Cliff Hotel were posted to Lyme Regis.

HSL 130 also rescued a bomber crew, the first pilot being "Sandy" Standford, who post-war served on the Westminster Council, London, and around June Flt/Sgt Flower MM, went on an "officer commissioning course".

HSL 130

It was from her shores that I first set sail
Into the teeth of a force nine gale.
I was to learn from an angry sea
What coping with life would mean to me.
The launch pushed on driving and fighting,
Battling her way it seemed exciting.
But launch and man were taking stick
It was not very long before I was sick.
My thought then turned to remustering
Man or mouse? This was not the thing
And of those out there who might die
At least I had a place for my head to lie.
That day for sure made a man of me
And ever since I have thanked the sea.
For there is nothing mightier if you pause to think,
Than those massive waves we called "the drink"
It can be calm and as smooth as glass
But when enraged you cannot pass
I am glad I went to sea that day
For I learned so much that I can repay
During that time a very short span,
I knew what it meant to be a man.

Charles Meacock, ex-Coxswain ASR

*HSL 130 (photo taken from HSL 132) offshore at Gorleston in early January 1942. [**Air Ministry**]*

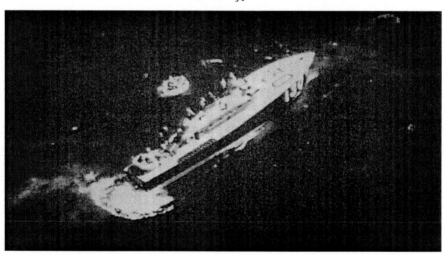

An SOS at 03.40 hours on 9th June 1942 from a Halifax of Bomber Command's No 4 Group alerted the air sea rescue crews of 279 Squadron. Six Hudson's took off in two waves from Bircham Newton heading towards the Netherlands. A yellow dinghy was spotted about 60 miles west of The Hague by Plt.Off. D. Boxhall, the air observer in the Hudson, flown by Sqn. Ldr Anthony F. Binks. The crew dropped a Lindholm dinghy (a large central dinghy with four smaller ones roped to it, containing supplies) but this did not inflate properly. A W/T message was sent to Bircham Newton and the other five Hudson's were soon circling the dinghy. At 10.35 hours RAF High-Speed Launch No 130 arrived from Yarmouth, and the men were taken to safety.

A TWO-LAUNCH CALLOUT.

There was great rivalry with the crew at Gorleston. Once the Klaxon had signalled a callout, the crews would dash to the launches, the fitters start up the engines, the coxswain would be on the helm and the wireless operator would open up on the rescue frequency.

*HSL 130 tied up at her Baker Street moorings,
her guns are visible either side of the bridge.*

Crew Members of HSL 130. *Back Row Left to right:-. LAC Lansbury, Nursing Orderly, LAC Warner MBC, Sgt Williams Fitter/Marine. LAC Saunders W.Op. Middle Row: LAC Brown MBC LAC Bryce W.Op LAC Pomery WEM. Front Row: LAC McClaren Fitter/Marine. Cpl Dave 2nd Coxswain. Photograph taken by Flt/Sgt Flower MM. 1st Coxswain [**C. Meacock**]*

6. Aground on Scoby Elbow – HSL124

It was not an auspicious start to the career of HSL124. She came up to Gorleston in early January and operated with both HSL130 and 132, but on 23rd January 1942 at 8.15 pm (20.15 hours) the Flag Officer in charge of Great Yarmouth asked through the Coastguards for the services of a lifeboat for the assistance of RAF HSL124, which was aground on Scoby Sands, north of the Scoby Elbow buoy. The Gorleston Lifeboat was preferred, as she was fitted with a wireless (the Caister Lifeboat was not).

A south south-west gale was blowing with a rough sea, rain, sleet and snow. The Gorleston Lifeboat *Louise Stephens* was launched at approximately 8.35pm (22.35 hrs) and found the launch on the Caister shoals. Trying to get alongside, the Lifeboat touched ground and had to put hard astern to back away.

The *Louise Stephens* then got into a position to fire her line-throwing gun, but at that moment a heavy sea knocked the launch afloat, and the tide now being on the flood, the Lifeboat was able to come alongside.

The Lifeboat then escorted her to Great Yarmouth harbour, after sending a message that the harbour lights be turned on as they came across the harbour bar, (very dangerous at this period of the war as Great Yarmouth and the harbour suffered constant attention from the Luftwaffe).

With the RAF launch safely moored up at the base, the lifeboat returned to her station at 11.40pm (23.40 hrs). The following morning, together with a message of thanks from the Flag Office, the crew received a bounty of 14 pounds, 16 shillings and sixpence.

The Gorleston Lifeboat "Louise Stephens" [The Williment Collection]

HSL 124 tied up at Baker Street after her clash with the Caister Shoals.

7. The End of the Beginning

The spring of 1943 saw the new 2000 Class HSLs arriving at 24 ASRU. The new designation was 'The Hants and Dorset' – after the well-known double-decker buses which operated in those counties. These HSLs were much taller than the whalebacks – 68 feet in length (5 feet longer) and a 17 feet beam, but their power and speed per knots was the same as the whalebacks.

The advantage they had over the previous boats was range – nearly 600 miles – and accommodation. The boats saved several ditchings per month, mainly from the 8th and 9th US Army Air Forces, which were building up to bomb "Festung Europe". Each rescue meant the saving up to ten souls from the B-17 Fortresses and Liberators, also the medium bombers, the B-26 Marauders from the 9th Air Force. Speckled amongst these were the RAF Bomber crews on their nightly missions to Germany. Fighter pilots, both RAF and USAAF and personnel from both the Royal Navy and the Kriegsmarine, together with Merchant Seamen of the coastal convoys, that plied their trade between the Thames estuary and the North-East ports of Tyneside and Newcastle, running the gauntlet of that most infamous piece of coast between Orfordness and Skegness – better known as "E-boat alley", right past the doorstep of 24 ASRU.

The new Air Ministry directive in 1943 also stated that to reduce the safety times to a rescue – and we all know that "speed is of the essence" – instead of waiting for call outs, a system of "rendezvous" was installed. This consisted of motor launches (both RAF and Royal Navy) going out on station to wait at sea on the bombers' return flight-path. Damaged aircraft of any nationality would know that if they put down in the sea, help would only be minutes away. This, coupled with the new airborne lifeboats, helped save many downed aircrews who would otherwise have perished in the cold North Sea.

Another essential task performed by both RAF and RN rescue craft was that of patrolling the *"Cuckoos"*. These were air sea rescue floats anchored in strategic locations in both the English Channel and the North Sea, close to the East Anglian Coast. Similar German air-sea rescue *"Lobster Pots"* had been anchored off the Dutch Coast during 1940/1941, and in January 1941 the Air Ministry agreed to build sixteen rescue floats of a similar pattern, to be moored at strategic points, and to be painted red and yellow, and to be equipped with food, clothing and blankets. They had cooking facilities and were fitted with a W/T and rescue flares.

No24 ASRU had three floats under their surveillance: ASR3, ASR6 and ASR10. These were moored at staggered intervals some 25 miles off the East Anglian coast and were serviced on a regular basis by both the Royal Navy and RAF rescue service.

It is interesting to note that after the capture of HSL108 in July 1941 she was acquired by the Luftwaffe to service their rescue floats. Whilst sitting it out in Stalag Luft 3, Roger Dagget, a crewmember of HSL108 who could speak German, saw in a propaganda magazine photographs of HSL108 in German service. She was being used for "pick ups" on the German *"Lobster Pots"*. The plotted course on a weekly basis was from Willelmshaven to Flushing (now Vlisengen) and return to Willelmshaven. This seems to be corroborated by many flight crews, who, on return to base, reported sighting an ASR launch operating off the Dutch coast.

In 1943 the boats at 24 ASRU had disappointments as well as success...

APRIL 22nd 10pm – A large number of American Liberator bombers were returning to their bases in darkness from a late afternoon raid on Hamm in Germany. They were attacked by Luftwaffe FW190s and ME410s which had followed them over the coast. In a 40 minute action, nine B24 Liberators were shot down, one crashing into the sea off Hopton at 10.07pm and one off Kessingland at 10.20pm – there were no survivors – only bodies were picked up and brought ashore.

MAY 27th   An Air Sea Rescue launch landed the bodies of five allied airmen [three RAF, one RAAF and one RNZAF] from an RAF Halifax bomber which had ditched 60 miles off Cromer. It had been on special duties (SOE).

Such were the disappointments, which meant live pick-ups were all the more to be savoured.

MAY 30th   At 1 pm a B24 Liberator which had been damaged by flak over Munster, ditched in the sea north of Lowestoft. The pilot brought the aircraft down near to some small fishing boats and after the crew had got clear, the bomber sank within 3 minutes. The radio operator released the life-rafts and nine of the crew were rescued by the fishermen. The tenth member, a gunner was unable to inflate his life preserver and was last seen clinging to the tail of the aircraft as it sank.

"Cuckoos nests" were moored life-rafts equipped with tins of food, dry clothing and a radio set on a fixed frequency directly to ASR Headquarters. They were inspected frequently by the RAF and the Royal Navy. Similar units were in use on the German side of the North Sea, where they were known as "Lobster Pots".

A Yarmouth-based Motor Gun Boat visits ASR10. Three of these unmanned life-rafts moored off the Yarmouth coast were the responsibility of the Gorleston craft.

*HSL 2550 making a pick up, of the rubber dinghy and showing its stabilisers which prevented it overturning in heavy seas. [**Air Ministry**]*

*HSL 2579 from No24 ASRU picking up survivors from an airborne lifeboat that had been dropped to them from one our aircraft. [**S.B.Daniels**]*

The US Eighth Air Force despatched 264 B-17 Flying Fortresses on a daylight raid to Hamburg on 25 July 1943 – 19 failed to return, some ditching in the North Sea. The ten-man crew of this Fortress had difficulties but an airborne lifeboat was dropped by a Coastal Commands Hudson. The crew climbed in, started the engine and set course for the English coast where they were met by HSL 2551 and escorted into Yarmouth.

HSL 2550 sister launch to the ill-fated HSL 2551.

New "2000" class HSL's (Hants and Dorsets) moored at
Baker Street Base 1943 **[S.B.Daniels]**

Two Airborne Lifeboat exercises off Gt Yarmouth and Gorleston
involving local HSLs and Naval RMLs.

HSL 185 no doubt travelling at maximum revs on a call out, she had a good record for pick-ups and saw her days out in the waters of Chichester Harbour, sold in 1946 to the Chichester Yacht Company.

HSL 180 moored alongside a "Hants and Dorset". Note the difference in the size of the superstructure.

8. "The Time Has Come", the Walrus Said

One must not forget the important ASR role played by the Supermarine Walrus, affectionately known to its crews as 'the Shagbat'. This was based on a 1933 design known as the Seagull Mk V, but a revamp of that design in 1935 resulted as the Walrus Mk1. It was a very rugged biplane with a single 'pusher' (rear-facing) engine, capable of being launched by shipborne steam catapults and thus ideal for air-sea rescue operations. In East Anglia one of the first ASR flights was set up at Martlesham Heath (277 Squadron, A flight) in 1941. This was followed by 278 Squadron at Matlaske (Sheringham) in 1943 and 279 Squadron at Bircham Newton in 1943.

On 25th July 1943, following a raid on Hamburg, several B17 Flying Fortresses from the US 8th Air Force were reported missing in the North Sea. A Hudson from 279 Squadron took off from Bircham Newton to look for one American crew off the Frisian Islands; en route he saw another aircraft in the sea off Cromer. He called for HSLs from 24 ASRU to the rescue, which saved the entire crew. Later another 279 Squadron aircraft sighted two more dinghies and two Walrus aircraft from 278 squadron were despatched, put down on the sea and rescued two more crews. Twenty seven airmen were saved on that day alone in a joint operation between air and marine services of the Royal Air Force.

However, not all Walrus rescues went according to plan... On 22nd June 1943 a complete 'shambles' was witnessed by the author off the coast of Caister Village. Although just a small boy at the time, the incident has remained indelibly etched on his mind ever since. An American P47 Thunderbolt and a Focke-Wulf 190 were engaged in combat over that part of the coast. The FW190 was the victor and the American pilot baled out. The author watched as the pilot descended into the North Sea off Barber Sands. After a period of time a Walrus arrived to pick up the pilot. It promptly ran aground on the Barber Sands. The Caister lifeboat was called, but as the tide was ebbing fast, it could not reach either the Walrus or the pilot. The rescue was eventually achieved by a small fishing boat crewed by Mr Beckett and Charles Newby from Scratby, who picked up the pilot and transferred him to the lifeboat. The lifeboat then stayed alongside until the tide began to flood and towed the Walrus into Great Yarmouth Harbour and onto Spending beach opposite 24 ASRU.

After checks and repairs she retuned to base the following day.

Crew Report
Data Copy 278 Squadron   26th July 1943
                                      RAF Coltishall

F/O Land – Pilot
P/O Scott – W/Op
WALRUS K 8549
"Quicksand" 6

"We were scrambled in the evening to an area 20 miles North of Cromer and on reaching the search position; we were met by our Anson and a Spitfire. The Anson dropped a smoke float and we located two American type dinghies each containing five men and a third empty circular dinghy, all tied together. The third dinghy was a Lindholme type which had been dropped with great accuracy by the Anson, in fact, almost a direct hit! Visibility was about 1½ miles with thick haze. The tide was running North to South but the wind was West to East and I anticipated that a take-off would have to be made running along the top of the swell. I landed at 8-50 hours in a moderate swell that was rapidly rising.

I taxied to the dinghies and found the ten men in good spirits and uninjured. They were eating the contents of the Lindholme containers and making use of the sleeping bags. We ascertained that they were a Fortress crew returning from Hanover. With the aid of our boathook, Scotty transferred five men to the Walrus and I attempted to take-off along the swell, but due the weight I could not get airborne. A second Walrus, pilot George Reeder, landed and took the other five crew members on board. The swell was getting nasty and after another unsuccessful attempt to take-off, Scotty said that he wasn't feeling very well and went to the back of the aircraft; I believe he was sick. I don't recall that he fainted and any first aid rendered was carried out by the Americans.

I watched George Reeder make his first attempt at take-off also along the top of the swell and it appeared to be a very hair-raising operation. He disappeared in clouds of spray into the haze and I thought he had become airborne, as I didn't catch sight of him again. I learned later that he too was unsuccessful due to the weight of the aircraft. I expected another Walrus to arrive to relieve us of some of our load and in the meantime prepared for another attempt at take-off. The swell had become heavy and as I turned across it, a wave came across the rear of the aircraft and tore a piece out of the starboard tail-plane. It was impossible to assess the damage, so I decided the only thing to do was get the hell out of it and taxi towards the coast.

We attached the two American dinghies to the struts on the wings of the Walrus and these were towed behind us. I followed a south-east course on the aircraft's compass and plodded on steadily. As it got dark, the swell subsided considerably and it was about midnight that Scotty reported that the aircraft was taking water. I had been taxiing for approximately four hours.

We thought that our own dinghy was floating in the aircraft. I ordered everyone to sit on the wings, three each side, and I opened the cockpit hatch to make a rapid escape should the aircraft capsize. We were ready to cut the two dinghies loose and occupy them in the event of an emergency.

From time to time I throttled back to listen for any outside activity. It was a dark, moonless night and on the horizon I could see a line of searchlights dipping from the vertical to the horizontal position, indicating the direction of Yarmouth. We could see aircraft in the distance also, but as I estimated that we must be in the shipping lane and what was known as the notorious 'E'-Boat Alley, we made no visual signals.

About this time water must have seeped into the electrical circuits because suddenly the cockpit and landing light came on. The landing lights shone like a great searchlight across a darkened sea. Scotty took a fire axe, edged along a wing and chopped it out. All the other lights went out at the same time.

As first light was dawning at about 03:00 hrs I saw a light approaching and we were intercepted by an HSL. The five rescued crewmen were transferred to the launch and I accepted a tow. The Pegasus engine had not faltered at any time and was behaving marvellously. The towing proved awkward as the aircraft was moving under its own power, a few miles from the coast we slipped the tow and following the rear light of the HSL, I taxied into the Royal Naval base at Gorleston, Great Yarmouth, where I lowered the undercarriage and ran up the beach, the time was 04:25 hrs. I estimated that I had been taxiing for eight hours at an average speed of about six knots – a distance of about 50 miles. There was about 18 inches of water in the hull. We were welcomed by the base Commodore and I was presented with an open bottle of whiskey, which both Scotty and I appreciated; we were both very cold and wet.

We were taken to the Base Mess, where in addition to our Fortress crew I think there were two other crews of 20 men that had been picked up by our launches the previous day. A merry party followed until a coach came and took all the Americans away. We were later taken by transport to Coltishall. A maintenance crew came from Coltishall; our aircraft was drained and the damaged tail repaired temporarily and in spite of a big mag drop when the engine was run up, the aircraft was floated and flown back to base without mishap. When the engine was later stripped down in the hanger the cylinders were thickly coated inside with dried salt.

Our Fortress crew had been flown back to their base when we returned to Coltishall but they had left me a French 50 franc note with their ten signatures on it. They were from 322 Squadron 91st Bomber Group.

Affectionately known as the "shagbat" the Walrus Amphibian was a game little aircraft to which a considerable number of airmen owe their lives. She was unusual in that she had a rear-facing 'pusher' airscrew. [**Air Ministry**]

Another view of the Walrus. [**Belsom**]

9. The RN Rescue Service at Great Yarmouth

No mention of No.24 ASRU would be complete without including its Royal Navy counterpart HMS *Midge* (the MTB/MGB base down-river) with which there was very close liaison and cooperation. Many friendships were made between the services, whose common aim was to rescue those in peril at sea.

The Royal Navy units usually consisted of four boats. These were adapted versions of the *Fairmile B,* but with a hospital unit on the stern in place of the Twin Oerlikon. Although slower than the RAF HSLs, they had the advantage of being larger, had more accommodation and could remain at sea longer in sustained searches. They were also much better boats in rough seas.

An incident involving cooperation between all rescue services (Royal Navy boats, air-sea rescue aircraft and RAF HSLs) was noted on July 26th 1943 following the great "fire raids" on Hamburg by the RAF at night, followed by the 8th USAAF by day. One of the 8th USAAF participants was B17 *"Weary Willie"* from the 544th Bomb Squadron, part of the 384th Bomb Group, based at Grafton Underwood. *"Weary Willie"* was the lead aircraft in the lower bomb group. After making their bomb run, they turned for home, but then their troubles began...

They were attacked by FW190s and twin-engined Messerschmitt 210s and 410s. After several attacks *"Weary Willie"* fell away from the main formation and, as a 'lame duck', was set upon by several fighters. The pilot, Lieutenant Estes, held his course and passed over the Danish Coast. They were still being attacked, three engines were hit and there was an explosion in the nose. There was no alterative but to ditch in the North Sea. The aircraft made a perfect "three-pointer" on a calm sea and all ten crew members took to their dinghies, six in one and four in the other. Thus they would remain for the next five hours until they were spotted by Lockheed Hudson 'U'-Uncle from No.279 Squadron, which dropped an airborne lifeboat with great precision, a mere 80 yards from the dinghies. The American crew paddled to it and got on board. After problems with the semi-outboard motor they put up the sail and were later picked up by HSL2551 from 24ASRU and taken back to the base at Gorleston.

The Royal Navy RML547 was already on call-out looking for three men in a dinghy off Ameland when they spotted the sail of a small fishing boat. Overhead, circling the craft, was an RAF Halifax Bomber. The skipper of the RML, Lt Andrews, decided to investigate further. When they approached they saw a crowd of American aircrew on board, who turned out to be the crew of B17 "Happy Daze" of 94th Bomb Group based at Bury St Edmunds. They had been part of a bombing raid on Kiel on 25th July when they were attacked by enemy fighters and ditched some 60 miles off the Danish Coast. They were in their dinghies, one of which had been damaged in combat, for some 36 hours when they were spotted by a Danish fishing vessel, the "Ternan" from Fredrickshaven, skippered by an elderly man with a boy for crew. On the deck was a large tarpaulin with "S.O.S. BRING BOAT" painted on it – and it was this that had alerted the Halifax. HSL184 was already on its way.

There are now two conflicting reports of subsequent events: one from the skipper of RML547, who stated that once the Americans were transferred aboard the Danes were given several cartons of cigarettes in exchange for a selection of fish. In Lt Andrews' words "This would make a welcome change for the galley instead of soya sausages and tinned greengages". The Danish fishing boat then cast off and headed back to its own port. The crew had been asked if they wanted to return to England, but fearing reprisals against their families, they elected to return to Denmark. The Americans were then transferred to HSL184 and brought back to Gorleston.

The second version is that the Danish fishing boat was returning to port (Fredrikshaven) with the Americans. The boat was intercepted and the Americans were transferred to HSL184. HSL2551 then escorted the Danish fishing vessel into Great Yarmouth and its crew were interned. Whilst this version may be true, the author can find no evidence to support it.

RML 547 then returned to her original search for the three men in a dinghy off Ameland, but to no avail. What had been proven, was that by co-operation between the Royal Navy rescue service and the Royal Air Force, both air and marine rescue services, that some twenty souls had been saved from the sea.

Although the Royal Navy boats rescued many RAF and other personnel from the North Sea, probably one of the most audacious rescues took place during operation 'Market-Garden' – the Arnhem offensive. RAF HSLs from Felixstowe, Lowestoft and Great Yarmouth together with their counterparts from HMS *Beehive*, HMS *Mantis* and HMS *Midge* were placed 'on station' (i.e. in stepped positions to cover any emergencies which might occur). The operation was one of the worst-kept secrets of the war, the heroics and disasters of which are well described by Cornelius Ryan in his book *A Bridge Too Far*.

During the night of 15/16th September 1944, in a flat-calm sea, all the rescue craft took up positions to attend any ditchings of aircraft or gliders. The Yarmouth flotilla, including Navy RMLs 520 and 498 were in the Scleldt estuary, so close inshore, they could see the Church Towers of both Domburg and Westkapelle, thus enabling them to get a perfect fix.

Overhead, aircraft in their thousands were passing when suddenly two gliders cast off their towropes and floated down into the sea. So quick was the rescue by RML 547 and an HSL from Felixstowe that the soldiers on board barely got their feet wet.

ASR Spitfires, Wellingtons and Warwicks, together with "Teamwork Thunderbolts" from the American air-sea rescue service were dropping smoke flares to mark the spot of ditched aircraft or gliders. One such fix was only a few hundred yards offshore on the northern tip of Walcheren Island. The glider was coming under intensive small arms fire and inshore battery fire. Under cover of fighter fire, RML 498 went in and rescued eight soldiers from the Parachute Regiment and the two glider pilots and returned them safely to Felixstowe. Five hours later they were back on station.

Operation "Market Garden" saw a number of gliders in the water, this example shows the identification marks painted on the wings and the dinghy with soldiers aboard waiting to be picked up.

The entrance and guard room to HMS Midge, home of the RMLs.

*The Royal Navy Rescue launch, good sturdy construction seen with
the hospital quarters aft of the funnel*

10. The Production Line

The East Coast was never famous for great dockyards like those on the River Clyde or Tyneside; just Chatham in Kent and a number of small yards on the Thames and Humber. But what we did excel at in East Anglia was expertise in building "Broads Cruisers" and other wooden boats, all built on traditional lines with bulkheads, stringers, diagonal timber cladding and suchlike – exactly the same specification that boat-builders like Vosper, Thorneycroft and British powerboat companies used to build Motor Torpedo Boats and High Speed Launches. It is little wonder then that during the war both the Admiralty and Air Ministry turned to some of these small and well-dispersed local yards to build for their requirements. Lowestoft was the largest centre, with companies like Brooke-Marine and Collins on Lake Lothing. Brooke-Marine had the contract to service and refit all the High Speed Launches from Gorleston and Lowestoft.

Further inland and within the Norfolk Broads were companies like Herbert Woods at Potter Heigham and H. Percival at Horning – it was one of Percival's boats (ML153) that attacked the midget submarine off Lowestoft in January 1945, so this was really a "local boat" – Graham Bunn's and Landamores at Wroxham and Broom's at Brundall. All of these small yards produced RAF HSLs and Pinnaces, Harbour Defence Launches (HDLs) and Royal Navy craft.

The large craft that were built up-river had to have their bridges and wheelhouses removed to negotiate Acle Bridge. The up-river builders jointly had a workshop next to Trinity Wharf, where the craft were completed. Herbert Woods had another workshop at Fisher's Quay (off North Quay) for the same purpose. Once completed these craft would head downriver, past 24 ASRU, to their eventual ports of destination.

Unfortunately, these activities did not go un-noticed by the enemy, and on the night of 27th April 1941 the Luftwaffe, looking for the yards at Wroxham, bombed the Horning 'Ferry Inn' public house, with severe loss of life. Nearly all the Sutton family were killed, together with a number of fighter pilots and RAF personnel from nearby RAF Coltishall. Herbert Woods' yard at Potter Heigham was also strafed by a lone aircraft, but with no serious damage. Such was the construction programme along the East

Coast that there were some 35 yards producing such vessels as Mine Sweepers (MMS) and Motor Fishing Vessels (MVFs), usually used as Harbour tenders.

All of these vessels were produced from wood, using traditional methods, both for speed of production and lower costs. Thus it was that this 'cottage industry' of cheap, efficient and traditional methods of boat-building made a major contribution to the war effort.

Another major innovation in saving life at sea was the advent of the air-borne lifeboat. I do not wish to enlarge on this, as the subject has been most adequately covered by Stephen Brewster Daniels in his book *Rescue from the Skies*. Suffice it to say that the initial idea of a lifeboat dropped from an aircraft came from Group Captain Waring, Officer Commanding at RAF Lindholme. He, together with Uffa Fox, the well-known racing yacht designer, and Lt Robb RNVR developed the project, with a big input from the local boat builder Herbert Wood, a long-time friend of Uffa Fox.

As Herbert Wood's Yard was only 15 miles up-river from 24ASRU, it was logical that some of the initial trials should be carried out by the Royal Navy (RMLs) and the Royal Air Force (aircraft from 279 Squadron at Bircham Newton and HSLs from 24ASRU) in the relative safety of the Great Yarmouth Roads.

Thus the East Anglian Boat Building industry contributed greatly to both the war effort and to saving life at sea.

RAF Pinnaces en-route for commissioning having left the builder yard, Herbert Woods Boat Yard at Potter Heigham, notice the bow waves. These were hard chine craft

GP Pinnace 1328 and 1327 passing the windmill on the River Thurne in transit, heading for bases to which they had been assigned.

An overall view of Herbert Wood's yard, showing four RAF Pinnaces under construction and two Harbour defence launches. The Harbour defence launches were manned by Royal Navy sailors. Note the gantry in the foreground used to load heavy weighted objects such as engines.

*An airborne Lifeboat at Herbert Woods' yard at Potter Heigham harnessed to a crane ready to lift and prepare for delivery to one of the ASR Airborne units. [**Photo courtesy of Jeanne Lee**]*

11. The Loss of HSL 2706

The third week in March 1944 saw a steady build-up of American 8th Air Force operations over Germany, especially with the advent of the new escort Fighter, the P51 Mustang, which was now coming into service in ever-increasing numbers.

On 23rd March 1944 the main bombing target was Brunswick. The return leg of the mission would take the bombers over Schouwen Island in the Scheldt Estuary. Air Sea Rescue Launches from Gorleston, Lowestoft and Felixstowe were to be on station to give assistance to any aircraft that ditched. Two such launches from 24ASRU were HSL2706 (F/O Mitchell) and HSL2679 (F/O Herrick)

The following is a report by F/O Herrick:

"Our boats were to take position along the line of the bombers' return. The most seaward boat was 2706, being some 30 miles from the enemy coast. I was in second position some ten miles to the North. We were in position by about 10.30am and watched the formations of Liberators and Fortresses return. Suddenly, at about 11.00am everything started to happen.

The Wireless Operator came to the bridge to report that HSL 2706 would not acknowledge a signal sent from HMS *Midge,* the Royal Navy base at Great Yarmouth. Then the RT set was aloud with an American voice saying that he was circling a burning boat. On the horizon to the south-east we saw a black smudge of smoke.

Then the radio broke again to summon my boat to the assistance of nine Americans from a Fortress from 94th Bomb Group, who had ditched and were in a dinghy. For the first and only time I disobeyed an order. I sent a signal to the next boat to pick up the Americans and headed flat-out towards the black smudge south-east of us. The American voice (an ASR Thunderbolt from Boxsted, Essex) kept up his hysterical commentary:

"Seagull 44 (the call-sign of 2679). Go down to identify numbers on the boat."

"OK Seagull 44, going down to check..."

"Hello Seagull 44. Confirm No 2706.

"Thanks OBOE 15 (the Thunderbolts call-sign). I shall be in position in 15 minutes."

The three throttle levers were pushed against the stops, producing 4500 revs. The boat was vibrating with power. We all knew "Mitch" and his crew and drank with them often at the Dock Tavern. Then more radio traffic – a B17 of 91st Bomb Group had ditched 15 miles to the East. We desperately asked for a Walrus from 277 Squadron at RAF Martlesham Heath to go to their rescue and search for survivors.

As we approached 2706 no words can describe the blazing fury of that fire – 1800 gallons of high octane fuel in a craft built entirely of wood. By the time we arrived the fire had eaten the boat almost to the waterline. A hundred yards down-wind we saw a Carley Float, almost down to the waterline, but as we drew near we could see only three survivors.

"Are you the only ones?"

"Yes."

"How many on board?"

"Thirteen."

"Are the rest killed?"

"Yes."

We drew them to our nets and realised that these three were far from unscathed.

Then another frantic message came over the RT:

"Oboe 15 – I've only got 15 minutes flying time – must leave – good luck".

I gave my wireless operator the following signal.

"HSL 2706 shot up – total loss – have picked up three survivors – returning base. ETA 1500 hrs. Medical aid urgent."

During the journey back to base Cpl Turner succumbed to his injuries and died. LAC Smallwood lost one arm and part of one leg. LAC Anderson survived, but never went to sea again. Of the thirteen men that went to sea that morning only two survived. But there remained the mystery – "Who shot up HSL 2706?" The shutters were pulled down, nobody would talk about the incident, and rumours prevailed. It wasn't until 2002, nearly 60 years on, that a chance meeting between Don Thurston of the Flixton Aviation Museum and a certain "Mr Smith" came up with answers, when he presented some photostat copies of the log sheets of 277 Squadron, "A" Flight, Martlesham Heath, and then the whole mystery was solved.

In early 1944 the American Army Air Force issued a directive to its Fighter Groups (Both 8th and 9th Air Force) that on return escort missions with the bombers, as long as the bombers were adequately protected, part of the fighter groups could go down and seek "targets of opportunity" (eg. flak-towers, locomotives, road transport and airfields).

Such was the case on 23rd March 1944 – P47 Thunderbolts from 356 Fighter Group based at Martlesham Heath were returning from escort duty; a Lt Col Tukey Jnr led the mission. When four pilots dropped down to do some strafing, Lt James B. Smith damaged a Messerschmitt 110 on the ground at Diest Schaffen airfield and then shared in the destruction of a locomotive with Capt E. White. Lt James Cook in P47 *Quirks Dark Horse* and F/O Shirley J. Green in P47 *Lone Star Lady* – "strafed and damaged an

E-Boat in the North Sea". Unfortunately, this was a case of mistaken identity; the so-called "E-Boat" was actually HSL 2706.

Owing to the presence of so many friendly aircraft in the vicinity the attack was totally unexpected. The Skipper, F/O Mitchell, was killed in the first pass, together with "Pop" Harding, who raised his head above the engine room hatch whereupon a round hit him in the face and took the back of his head off. He fell back into the engine room. Anderson got to the Oerlikon and got off a quick burst. "Ginger" Smallwood got out of the engine room and ran towards the wheelhouse, but most of the crew, who were on deck, died in the first pass.

Anderson, somehow, with superhuman strength managed to launch the Carley Float. He then returned to the now burning wheelhouse to rescue Cpl Turner. Passing the wireless cabin he grabbed a fire extinguisher to battle the flames when an explosion caught both him and LAC Smallwood and lifted them out on deck. They got Cpl Turner into the Carley Float but after this the launch became a mass of flames. Anderson carried out a fine job launching the Carley Float and rescuing Smallwood and Turner. He received serve burns whilst doing this.

The RAF Air Sea Rescue service was held in high esteem amongst the American Air Force, both the 8th and 9th in Europe and indeed across the world. The incident was witnessed by one Lt Wilkinson, a P38 Pilot from 364th Fighter Group, based at Honington, who followed the Thunderbolts back to Martlesham Heath, landed, and made a full report to the CO. He was so angry, that he was on the point of crying.

Both the Thunderbolt Pilots, F/O Green and Lt Cook had to go before a Court of Enquiry. Lt Cook was killed on operations 18th July 1944, and F/O Green returned to the States in July 1944.

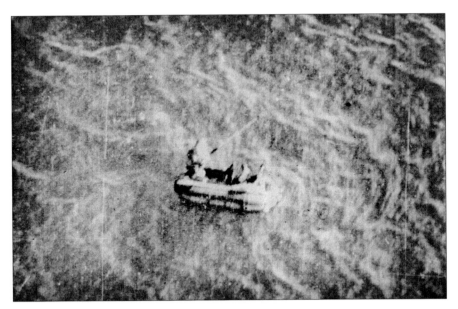

Crew members Cpl Turner, LAC Smallwood and LAC Anderson of HSL 2706 in the Carley Float.

First of a series of photographs showing the demise of HSL 2706 after being attacked by a P 47 Thunderbolt. Taken by an RAF Warwick of 279 Sqdn, Bircham Newton.

HSL 2706 fully ablaze

*HSL 2706 launch now burned down to the waterline [**Air Ministry**].*

A tribute to the crew of HSL 2706

They were ordered to sea t'was a bright sunny day,
Not a cloud in the sky as they sped on their way.
The rendezvous point was off the Dutch Coast,
Where they awaited the return of the Flying Fort host
They lay on the foredeck drinking their tea,
Chatting away about the bright sunny day
And the delights of having a very calm sea.
More often than not the North Sea was wild,
It made quite a change to have it so mild.
But trouble was coming and they did not know this,
A fighter plane swooped, he was not our foe.
An American fighter plane opened fire with his guns,
Killing ten of the crew on the first of his runs.
He came in again with all guns blazing,
Setting fire to the launch, the carnage amazing.
There were only three left alive, fighters drove him away,
And with no time to lose if the three were to live.
A float had to be launched with all the strength he could give,
by the one conscious man God had permitted to live.
A short distance away from the inferno, his load,
When eighteen hundred gallons of petrol was about to explode.
She burnt to the waterline cremating her dead,
A rescue launch came and picked up the three.
Set maximum revs for Gorleston-on-Sea.
Where medics were waiting to care for one lad,
Whose arm was all shattered and his right foot as bad.
But a coxswain who had lived with shells in his back,
Gave up the ghost as they dashed for the Yare,
For them only to find wife and baby were there.
The lad had seen this whole ordeal through,
Stepped ashore among friends but what could they do?
The C.O. then greeted him, well done my young man,
Corporal, see what he wants and do what you can.
What a hero this man put his friends before self
No medals, or gongs, he was shore based for good
To regain both his mental and physical health.

by Charles Meacock ex ASR Coxswain

12. The Loss of HSL 2551

Outwardly there was not much to distinguish High Speed Launch 2551[2] from the other boats of the No.24 Air Sea Rescue Unit based at Gorleston-on-Sea in the summer of 1943, except, perhaps, that indefinable air which an exceptional skipper and a fine crew give to any craft fortunate enough to possess both. The River Yare was very different from four to five years previously when holidaymakers had thronged its banks and the double ended "Lily" boats with crowded decks had plied between Great Yarmouth's Town Quay and Gorleston's Brush Quay.

There were no brightly clad visitors now, only the drabness of khaki, navy blue and the brighter, but rarer, Air Force blue, not that the cluster of wooden huts on the waterside corner of Bakers Street sported much satirical elegance, denim overalls, thick woollen white jerseys and heavy sea boots were much more in evidence. The "Brylcreem" was only seen to come out on special occasions, for this was not the home of the glamorous fighter pilots but salt-hardened seamen who defied all conditions to rescue their unfortunate comrades.

There's no romance in being aboard a "Crash Boat". Tragedy was a frequent attendant, when injured men and lifeless bodies had to be recovered from the sea, which made the occasions of "live" pickups matters of general satisfaction. Relaxation could not be allowed until after a safe return to harbour, followed by a quiet celebration in the bars of the "Belle Vue", "The Lifeboat" or the nearby "Dock Tavern". (Jerry had flattened RNLI Lifeboat Cox'n Joe Johnson's even nearer "Waterside Tavern" some time previously.)

All day, and much of the night, the river's turgid ebbs and cleaner floods of tides were stirred by the thrashing propellers as BYMSs, Fleet and Trawler Mine Sweepers, Motor Torpedo Boats, Motor Gun Boats, Royal Navy Motor Rescue Launches, Service Drifters, Merchant Ships and a host of other wartime marine traffic passed up and down between the parallel

---

[2] HSL2551 was one of the 29 or so Royal Air Force High Speed Launches stationed at Gorleston at various times during the war, a 63ft double diagonal mahogany-planked 'whaleback' craft built by the British Power Boat Company, displacing 28 tons, fitted with three 500 horsepower Napier Sea Lion petrol engines and able to carry a crew of 11, their supplies and armaments plus 1,800 gallons of high-octane fuel. It had a maximum speed of 38.5 knots, a cruising speed of 23.5 knots and a range of 580 nautical miles.

three miles of open quays, always under the watchful Bofors on their riverside flak towers, for Jerry was a frequent hit-and-run visitor.

2551 was only a youngster in age but a veteran in experience, for after entering service on 13th November 1942 she'd had a brief working up period at Calshot before a short posting to Leuchars in Scotland, after which she moved south to the centre of what was probably the busiest Air Sea Rescue area in Europe – between Cromer and Felixstowe – with only Gorleston and Lowestoft based boats to cover a 90-mile stretch of coast, with an area which extended to the enemy shores only one hundred or so miles to the east. Further round the bulge of Norfolk the service was represented at Wells-next-Sea and further north were the bleak areas of the North Sea with the next base at Grimsby on the River Humber.

The three bases at Gorleston, Lowestoft and Felixstowe covered the flight paths of the majority of the RAF and USAAF Bombers as they harried and pounded Germany by night and day. Inside the sandbanks all along the coast from Cromer to Orford Ness was the notorious "E-Boat Alley" where the intrepid "S" and "R" raiders lay awaiting convoys of merchant ships, unwary sweepers or crash boats. Aided by the Navy's Motor Gun Boats, which hunted the hunters, this was the gauntlet which had to be run twice on every operation. In the clouds above lurked the Luftwaffe, watching for lone or lightly-armed craft which might provide a 'target of opportunity'.

Flight Lieutenant George Lindsay was not only a good skipper, he was apparently a lucky one, frequently managing to be in the right area at the right time, guided, of course, by the Operations Rooms of Coastal Command HQ with its Controllers and WAAFs. His record was top line with a list of outstanding operations.

The winter brought a diminution of aerial activity, so the HSL crews spent rather less time at sea, but the hours at sea were in far worse conditions. The boredom of waiting at a rendezvous for a signal was bad enough, but to have to spend the long dark hours being mercilessly thrown about in freezing conditions called for stoicism and dedication of a very high degree.

During the following May (20th) a report of a Flying Fortress ditched well to the Danish side of the Dogger Bank brought out search aircraft of 279 Squadron from Bircham Newton at 1557 hours and onwards. The mainly Canadian crew in 279K, under F/O Reade, were the first to sight the survivors and drop a lifeboat to them at 1822 hours. After watching the ditched airmen board it and set a course of 250 degrees at 1835 hours, the aircraft had to return to base, due to shortage of fuel, but a Warwick Aircraft maintained surveillance until darkness fell.

In the early light at 0600 on the 21st, three Danish trawlers approached the lifeboat, one taking the men aboard and the boat in tow, before setting a course towards the South Western Coast of Denmark. W/O Oakes in a watching plane signalled them to change course and put a bust of machine gun fire across their bows to emphasise the point. This brought all three vessels to a stop and so they remained under the watchful eyes of the pilots of four P47s of the USAAF Emergency Squadron.

At half past nine HSL 2551 arrived and took the survivors aboard, arriving back at Gorleston at 16.40 hours. The rescued men were from an aircraft of the 100 Bomber Group, piloted by Lt J.R. Rogers USAAF. He reported being very hospitably received by the Danes who were prepared to stay in the area for two days to await the arrival of the unexpected rescue craft.

Already the Royal Navy and the RAF had won a famous reputation in occupied Europe for attempting long and dangerous missions, and using every ingenuity and effort to rescue ditched airmen – regardless of nationality. It is worth noting the virtual air superiority the Allies had achieved over the North Sea by this time, and also the different tactics employed by allowing the Dutch Vessels to fish unhindered, whereas German "hit and run" raiders were attacking and sinking single unarmed fishing vessels, lightships and even Lifeboats.

June 29th 1944 was a fateful day for the Air Sea Rescue Services and tragically illustrates the hazards which had to faced, apart from the weather. Warwick's "Q" and "G" of 280 Squadron were sent to a position 150 miles ESE of Flamborough Head in an unsuccessful search for eight men of a Flying Fortress "E for Easy" of the 390th Bombardment Group reported to be adrift in two dinghies. HSL 2551 had meanwhile made a pick up many miles away from the reported position and taken the survivors on board to make all speed back to its No.24 Air Sea Rescue Unit at Gorleston. This was the day HSL 2551's luck ran out and its outstanding career came to an end.

It would appear that the position given to the Warwicks was not at all accurate, for HSL 2551 was still very close to the Dutch Coast after picking up its human cargo when it was attacked by enemy planes believed to be Me210 or Me410 aircraft from KG51 Gilze-Reine and set on fire. Some of its crew and the survivors were killed and several others injured. As HSL 2551 burned down to the waterline and sank the remaining fifteen men took to the launches Carley float and various other dinghies, soon to be alone in the grey wilderness, wounded and wet, cold and dispirited, in the fading daylight.

The official enquiry revealed the Flt Lt Lindsay and his crew of HSL2551 were not actually on duty when the news came through about the Flying Fortress crew, but learning that the other crash boats were already out after other ditched airmen, he called his men together and soon their plumed wake was heading out between the piers, leaving the pulled-aside Naval boom wallowing in their wake.

The Coast of East Anglia is fringed by offshore sandbanks with "gats" or channels through which vessels can pass to reach the relatively open water. Some of these shoals dry out at low water, especially with the twice-monthly spring tides, whilst others, treacherously hidden, await unsuspecting passing vessels. The local fishermen and lifeboatmen knew the gats well, but HSL2551, drawing just four feet of water, would have to keep to the major mineswept fairways before setting course at maximum speed for the new position just off the coast of Holland.

With some minor trepidation Flt Lt Lindsay unhesitatingly took his craft and crew into the protective minefield where the USAAF men from a B17 of 390 Bomb Group were helpless in their two dinghies. When 2551 had set out it was a fairly familiar sort of southern North Sea day, not too much wind but gentle swells, a sufficient reminder of an earlier breeze to give a bumpy ride.

Overhead the usual slight haze was thin enough for the two escorting USAAF fighter to maintain contact, but not sufficient for an enemy aircraft to hide in, although there can be little doubt that the operation was being watched from a discreet distance. So all went well and the pick-up was successfully completed in a rather choppy sea, for by now the wind had freshened and brought in thicker clouds. These were fairly high, but with no sea mist to conceal the wake of the HSL heading for home with eight rescued Americans and a couple of escorting fighters to keep the wolves at bay.

Before long the escorting fighters were forced to leave because endurance had been reached and their replacements were not yet in evidence. But their departure was not unobserved and one of the wolves, in the form of an enemy plane, sized the opportunity to strike, and within a few minutes came diving down with all guns blazing. In the initial attack

HSL2551 was not only rendered helpless but also shattered and set ablaze from stem to stern.

Those who could, took to the water, but one American and one of the HSLs crew were killed and seven were badly wounded. With the remaining half of his total complement assisting, Skipper Lindsay led the efforts to get the wounded onto anything which would float sufficiently to support them and was last seen swimming to fetch a dinghy which had drifted a little distance away.

Other HSLs from Gorleston were also active in the eastern part of the North Sea, for there had been a heavy RAF raid the previous night. They picked up the brief attack report which the "sparks" had been able to get off. Immediately two of them – 158 and 184 – headed for the area and were fortunate in making a quick sighting, which enabled them to take fifteen survivors from the cold waters and pick up the body of Flt Lt George Lindsay, who had died of exposure in his gallant effort to retrieve the errant dinghy. All were later landed at Great Yarmouth, some spending considerable time in the Royal Naval Hospital there. Flt Lt Lindsay's body was landed at HMS *Miranda*, the trawler-sweeper unit, just across the river from where the RAF boats berthed.

At the subsequent official enquiry, the eyewitness reports failed to establish just when and how the fatalities occurred; all that could be known was that the B17 Navigator 2nd Lt J.S. Mayall was drowned swimming from one life-raft to another. The Ball Turret Gunner, Sgt G.S. Downie was killed aboard HSL2551, as were three of the launch's crew. Flt Lt Lindsay was lost at sea and the others were wounded by gunfire. The total casualty list from the aircraft and the boat was 12 men, either dead or wounded. Some witnesses said there were 15 Americans aboard, which beggars the question "Could this have been a double pick up?" It was also learned that the actual rescue position was so close to Ijmuden harbour that the helmets of the German soldiers could be seen on the harbour wall, so that the survivors in the dinghies would have been in plain sight, yet no shots were fired at either the dinghies or the RAF launch during the rescue.

At HMS *Miranda* an honour guard of four sailors with reverse weapons was posted round the bier and the entire base came to attention when, at 0130 hours, two days later, an HSL came alongside to accept its sad load and lead the cortège to sea. It was a fine crisp day, with a light south-westerly breeze as the convoy threaded its way out between the sandbanks and the protective minefields to rendezvous some miles off the coast.

Aboard the accompanying HSLs with a Naval Rescue Motor Launch, a Motor Torpedo Boat and a Motor Gun Boat in attendance, were the survivors of HSL2551, who were only dubiously well enough to attend, many of Lieutenant Lindsay's friends, other 24 ASRU skippers, high-ranking Coastal, Fighter and Bomber Command officers, a very senior USAAF officer and Naval officers from the three Great Yarmouth Bases of HM ships *Watchful, Midge* and *Miranda*. As the boat stopped engines, the other craft formed a circle around her and joined in the committal service, re-starting their engines in turn to pass slowly by, to cast their tributes at the spot where the first wreaths floated, whilst overhead, three Coastal Command Warwicks led a dipping salute flypast, followed by three United States Flying Fortresses and three Thunderbolt Fighters.

Author's comments

1. The official report into the destruction of HSL 2551 states that it was carried out by Junkers Ju88 aircraft. Most of the *Zerstorer* or fighter units with this aircraft were stationed on the Atlantic Coast of France to cover the Bay of Biscay. The night fighter versions had been pulled back behind behind the 'Kamhuber Line', an imaginary line running approximately along the Dutch German Boarder. This was to combat the nightly raids made by Bomber Command. The Author was therefore surprised that the official reports stated that the Launch was shot up by Ju88s. It is highly unlikely that any bomber units would undertake such a task.

In June 1995 there was a reunion between one of the B17 crew that was rescued and the former Coxswain of HSL2551, Harry Stamp. The American was Bob Gillmore from Indiana, who was the tail gunner, and during the course the conversation, they discussed the type of aircraft that shot them up. Bob Gillmore stated quite categorically that they were Messerschmitt 410s. As a Gunner, he and his crew's lives would depend on instant aircraft recognition. The author then started to delve deeper and contacted his main German source, whose information is always well researched.

In May 1944 German Fighter Bomber Group KG51, which had been flying Me410s on the Russian Front, had been pulled back to Gilze-Reine in Holland. Their prime task was to break up the concentrated American formations with RZ 65 under wing air-to-air rockets. Gilze-Reine is only approximately four minutes flying time from Ijmuiden. The initial pick-up by HSL2551 was only some three miles off the coast of Ijmuiden in full view of the German shore batteries.

The official report states quite clearly that the Germans could see the launch. It seems logical therefore that the Germans witnessing this pick-up would "whistle-up" the nearest Luftwaffe unit – Gilze-Reine. More practicable than calling up a Junkers 88 unit based 100 miles away.

KG51 was based at Gilze-Reine from May until September 1944 when it converted onto the new Messerschmitt 262 jet fighters.

2. The Official Enquiry failed to establish how or when the fatalities occurred, indeed it was reported that 1st Lt E.W. Moody was killed in the ditching, this was not the case. Lt Moody was rescued by one of the other HSLs from Gorleston, and went on to fly another 24 missions, including the last bombing mission to Schweinfurt. 1st Lt (later Captain) Moody flew his last mission on 12th October 1944 before returning to America – a grand total of 33 combat missions.

The B 17 G in question was built in Vega USA, Serial No 297830. It operated in the UK as aircraft "E" Easy, with 571 Bomber Squadron of the 390th Bomber Group at Parham (Framlingham) Suffolk.

The target on the 29th June was Bohlen in Germany, some 20 miles south of Leipzig. After the bomb run and on the return leg home, the aircraft was hit in the number 2 engine by flak, as it neared the Dutch coast it had to feather two more engines, and consequently had to ditch in the North Sea, west of Ijmuiden.

The crew of B17 Flying Fortress 'E' Easy were:

Captain	1st Lt E.W. Moody
2nd Pilot	W.H. Nugent
Navigator	2nd Lt J.S. Mayall
Engineer	D. Beeson
Bombardier	D.R. Simpson
Radio/Op	W. Bell
Ball Gunner	Sgt D. Downie
Tail Gunner	R. Gillmore
R/Waist Gunner	C Gray
L/Waist Gunner	F. Zanetti

HSL 2551 crewmembers killed in action:

F/Lt G Lindsay	Skipper
Cpl J.G. Stewart	MBC
LAC P.G. Sykes	MBC
LAC D. Wood	W/OP

*Flight Lieutenant George Lindsey and his crew, seen walking across the lawn at the rear of the Cliff Hotel Gorleston. Their launch HSL 2551 was the last of the series of Whalebacks to be built [**Air Ministry**]*

*Four of the Officers serving on the base just before the time when the shooting up of HSL 2551 took place. Left Flight Lieutenant P. Field, with Flight Lieutenant G. Lindsay third from left. [**courtesy of P. Field.**]*

A nautical farewell to Flight Lieutenant George Lindsay. His body was sewn in canvas and carried on an HSL, escorted by other HSLs and friends from the Royal Navy aboard their launches, which were also based at Gorleston.

The crew of HSL 184, based at Gorleston during 1942, depicting skipper 'Nobby' Clarke and Flight Sergeant Harry Stamp, who was coxswain aboard HSL 2551 on the occasion she was shot up and sunk, an indication of how interchangeable HSL crewmembers were.
[courtesy of H. Stamp]

13. The Ditching

by Robert Gillmore, tail gunner on B-17 "E" EASY

The date was 29 June 1944. Don Downey, our ball turret gunner and I were temporarily detached to Lt Edgar Moody's crew (571) to replace two of his crew members who were ill. Thankfully, this only happened once. I wasn't very happy about it, believing our pilot, Fran Maher, to be the tops in the squadron. Happily, my concerns were unfounded, Lt Moody showed us that he was a first-class pilot also.

I don't recall any details of the mission briefing regarding the flak or fighters. It was probably "normal", meaning there were no heavy concentrations of unavoidable flak on the path in or out. The target was the synthetic oil refinery at Bohlen, Germany. I had not been there before, but their refineries were always well covered by flak, both stationary and the unpredictable rail-mounted mobile type.

Early in our combat tour a flight group had two and three-plane echelons in each of the high, lead and low squadrons (18 plane group). The lead position of the high echelon of the high squadron must have been an absolute bear to fly without drifting out of formation or having a collision (I saw one happen while outbound near London). Later on, only the lead squadron had two echelons, with just one echelon in the high and low squadrons (12 plane group).

On this mission we were in No.830, positioned (I think) in the left wing of the high squadron's upper echelon (an 18 plane group). The mission progressed "normally" through the Initial Point (IP) of the bomb run. Flak was, as always *TERRIYFING* (for me) from the IP to the drop. Early in the bomb run one round of barrage went off very close underneath us (extremely loud), but we seemed OK. Shortly afterwards though, Lt Moody pulled out of the formation, encountering some vortex turbulence on the way that nearly turned us upside down.

After returning to our position Lt Moody told us that we had lost No.3 engine, but said we would be able to stay in formation on the remaining three engines and continue the bomb run.

Apparently the co-pilot "clutched up" and Lt Moody had to pull out of the formation so he could perform the prop feathering procedure and fly the plane himself (unconfirmed). Thankfully, Lt Moody was a cool and competent pilot.

We stayed in formation through the drop and for a while afterwards. Then Lt Moody told us that because we had lost No.4 engine and could no longer keep up. Apparently the close flak burst had done some latent damage, probably to the oil coolers. We had P-38 escorts on this mission and some of them stayed with us as we fell behind and began descending.

With close fighter escort we didn't need on-board armament as much as we needed to lose weight. We were told to dump everything we could in order to lighten the plane and stretch our glide. I pulled my two guns and threw them out of the little tail position window (very small on a B-17G). The ammo belts were more difficult, but thinking about the alternative somehow gave me the needed motivation!

I don't know our height or position when No.1 engine began to fail. Lt Moody said we could probably make it to the Dutch coast and ditch if our No.2 engine stayed healthy. He later said he overrode the limit stop and set the turbocharger to maximum overboost. (No need to worry about abusing an engine that was shortly going to be sitting on the bottom of the North Sea.)

We cleared all loose materials from the radio room and we five "back end" gunners gathered there. The radio room skylight was removed and pitched overboard. Through some training oversight Lt Moody's crew had not been trained in ditching. Fortunately, Don Downey (the ball gunner on loan with me from Maher's crew) and I had been trained.

We were sitting on the radio room floor in the appropriate positions as we crossed the Dutch coast. We must have been fairly low. I heard a lot of crackling noise, then, I noticed wood splinters from the waist area catwalk flying into the air. Finally it dawned on me that this was small-arms fire from the German infantry on the ground. Fortunately there were no skeet shooters among them! They didn't lead us far enough to hit anyone, or any critical parts. The shooting stopped as we moved out to sea.

The sea was relatively calm and the weather was 'benign' (or I wouldn't be writing this). Lt Moody did a fantastic job of ditching. We bounced off the top of a swell doing about 95 (I was told later). The noise was absolutely awesome. The plane flew onward for a while and I saw that that the waist compartment entrance door was torn off. Then it sounded like *THE WORLD HAD COME TO AN END!*

When I got my head above water I was standing in the middle of the bomb bay about 5 feet forward of the radio room. I remembered flipping end over end, but had no recollection of crashing through the closed wooden door from the radio room to the bomb bay. My mouth was full of seawater and I'd evidently swallowed quite a bit, but otherwise I seemed OK.

Water was about waist high but the plane seemed stable. The other crew were making their way out through the radio room skylight. In our ditching training we were told to expect the plane to sink in as little as 30 seconds. With that in mind it didn't take long to make my way from the bomb bay, through the splintered door into the radio room.

Everyone had stayed in the radio room and was ahead of me getting to the sky light exit. They all seemed to be moving as slow as molasses in January. I recall babbling like an idiot saying, "Plenty of time... Lets go!" over and over again. This must have aggravated somebody who said, "Shut up, dammit! We are going as fast as we can!"

Finally it was my turn to be hoisted up through the skylight and out onto the left wing. By this time the life raft compartments were open and the rafts inflated. For some reason I noticed that the two visible propeller blades of No.2 engine (running at maximum over-boost) were wrapped back round the cowl like strips of sealing tape on a package.

Pleased with our survival, we were in an almost light-hearted mood as we got into the rafts and paddled away from the plane. It was only then I became aware that my left elbow hurt like the dickens. Lt Moody asked if anyone was hurt. Don Downey (my crew mate) said his ankle was sprained. A couple of others had some dings and I reported my elbow. On balance not a bad outcome, considering all things that realistically could have happened.

The P-38 fighters orbited as we sat watching the plane bobbing up and down in the water. My estimate is highly suspect, but it seemed as if good old 830 stayed afloat for at least 10 minutes. The tail rose up, slowly at first and then with increasing speed to perhaps 30 degrees when it rather gently slid under – an emotional experience to see it go. It was a good airplane. I believe it was built by Vega.

While waiting for the air-sea rescue boat we all sat there quietly, in reasonable comfort, not saying much. I looked at the Dutch coast and saw what appeared to be power poles clearly visible. I don't recall any other details. I don't really know how far off the coast we were, but it was probably 5 to 6 miles. I wish I'd had enough sense to ask the rescue crew for an estimate.

The air-sea rescue boat (from Great Yarmouth, I think) came sweeping up like a PT boat on attack and looked absolutely terrific! The British crew cheerily helped us aboard and (fortunately) also brought our rubber life rafts on board as well. We deflated and removed our Mae West life vests and began trying to relax, believing that the worst was behind us for the day.

I didn't notice it at the time, but apparently our fighter escort left us then, probably short on fuel, as they had provided mission escort for the group. As far as I know they were not replaced – bad news for us...

Don Downey's ankle was hurting badly by then, perhaps broken, so he was taken forward to lie down on a bunk. I stayed in the boat's mid-ship cabin with the rest of the crew. They were all beginning to talk freely now, but since I was a stranger I wasn't included.

After a short period (less than half an hour) there was a lot of noise and stuff started flying around in our compartment. Obviously the Luftwaffe was strafing us. I grabbed a small tin bucket (about 8 inches diameter) and held it in front of my head, although tt wouldn't have stopped a .22 target round, much less a 20mm! After two strafing passes, they left. We all scrambled out on deck. One of the British crew said a pair of Me 410s had attacked us.

The boat was beginning to burn up front. The young Englishman that operated the mid ship Oerlikon 20mm anti-aircraft cannon was sprawled dead on the deck. He looked to be in his teens. I remember thinking that he sure had bright red hair, then realizing it was his blood. The power machine gun turret up forward was also badly shot up. I didn't see what happened to the gunner, but he surely didn't survive.

With the boat stopped dead in the water and now burning more briskly it was obvious that we had to get off. We scrambled to find our life vests and fortunately most of them still had air. We had deflated them when we took them off and now had to blow them back up with lung power. We hadn't deflated the rubber life-rafts, but the 20mm had pretty well shot up ours (and the ones on the rescue boat).

I asked one of the British crew about Don Downey (forward cabin) and was told he had taken a 20mm in the head. In retrospect I wish I'd gone to see for sure, but the boat was burning up there and an explosion seemed eminently possible. Thankfully it never did blow, continuing to burn with a highly visible black smoke plume that helped save us.

There were three or four rafts which at least one compartment the held air. We pitched them overboard and used them to hold onto, as they couldn't actually, carry anyone on board.

This was a real "downer" for us all. I asked one of the boat crew if a radio call had been made and what our chances were of being picked up. He said, "Not good mate. Radio's shot up and we're well off the beaten path". From his statement and manner it seemed likely that we were history. The North Sea, even on a good day in June, has a fairly brief survival time-interval.

It was so dammed cold that we all became extremely lethargic, like a bunch of lizards on a cold day. First my shoes and later my socks fell off, probably from the movement of treading water. I distinctly remember feeling that my toes were freezing and falling off also, one by one, as I moved my feet. For some fool reason, that seemed to bother me more than the possibility of drowning.

I vaguely heard one of the Americans calling out "Help me!" over and over again. I looked at him, without any real comprehension, and saw he was about 15-20 feet away. In a dream-like sequence it seemed that he was drifting away at about walking speed, as if he was being dragged by some sea creature.

Probably because of the intense cold none of us took any action to help, even if we could. He obviously drowned, though no one I talked with later could recall any details. Certainly not one of our more noble moments, a fact that bothers me to this day.

It turns out this was Lt James Mayall, the Navigator. His wife and parents lived in Long Beach (CA) near my home. I visited them when I got back to the US on furlough; a stressful experience but it was their only chance to hear what had happened. It didn't seem appropriate to tell them the shameful truth that none of us even tried to help him, whether or not we could have actually done anything.

I heard later that shortly after we went into the water Fred Zanetti, the Waist Gunner, dived down to save one of the boat crew who had been wounded and was losing consciousness. He surely would have drowned, otherwise. Fred's Dad and mine both worked at Douglas aircraft in Long Beach, CA and made contact as a result of the ditching (a copy of a news article from my Grandmother's rural paper detailed this).

The boat continued to burn without exploding, sending up a prominent black smoke plume. It was probably noon, or after, when we heard an aircraft. I vaguely thought, "The bastards are coming out to finish us off". Somehow, though, that didn't really seem to be particularly important.

It was a single-engined fighter and it looked as if would pass over us at about 5,000 feet without turning. Finally it turned, descended and made a low pass by the (thankfully) still burning boat. It was still too far away to recognise what kind of plane it was.

Happily he must have spotted our partially submerged yellow life rafts and made a couple of low passes nearby. The plane had a radial engine and bubble canopy. Didn't appear to fit the recognition profile of any US fighter – maybe British, or German? Then, on another low pass, I could see it was a new P-47 with a bubble canopy (I had never seen one before). As loudly as I could (not very) I shouted "It's ours!" just as others on our raft also made the recognition.

He apparently radioed for help and in a while (20-30 minutes) another P-47 arrived with some kind of a tube attached under the belly. He made some low passes and on the last one something dropped from the belly. It landed only about 40-50 feet from our raft and upon hitting the water it inflated and we could clearly see that it was a fairly large round life raft (with no holes!).

But we were still so lethargic that none of us made any kind of move towards it; instinctively the inflated life raft we were hanging onto seemed more secure than a bigger one 50 feet away.

Believe me, to this day I have a very warm feeling for that P-47, but tragically we never had (took?) the opportunity to thank our many anonymous benefactors.

My elbow was really beginning to hurt (bruised and minor bone chip) and in an intellectual fog I somehow decided I had to get out of the water or I wouldn't make it. Pointing to the new raft I said to Lt Moody, "I'm going to try to get it. If I don't make it will you come and get me?" It was a dumb question, and I knew it. At that point nobody was capable of helping anyone else, regardless of their desires.

I took off, doing a very slow one-handed dog paddle. It seemed like the exercise helped to revive me. I made it to the raft but was too worn out to do more than hold onto the side for a while. Finally, I realised that I couldn't hold on much longer. I had either to get into the raft or give up and go under. I was so cold that the decision seemed detached and almost academic; it felt as if I were just a mildly interested observer at the event.

Getting in was awkward with only one functional arm, but I finally made it. Looking back to the raft I'd come from I saw that the rescue pilot had done an absolutely fantastic job of dropping the raft, there was a line from my raft to a string of brightly coloured floats that terminated about six feet from the partially inflated raft the others were still using.

I shouted to them and motioned toward the end float only a few feet away from them. Their actions showed that they could see and hear me, but with the cold they couldn't comprehend, I tried paddling my raft towards them with my functioning right hand, but it was a round raft and all it did was rotate. I sat for a moment and must have passed out. I don't remember anything more until the second air-sea rescue crew grabbed my shoulders to drag me on board.

A physician had flown out to us in a Walrus flying boat to take any seriously injured back. By this time it was afternoon and the sea swells were getting stronger. They were so high that the flying boat couldn't take off and had to taxi all the way back to Great Yarmouth on the surface. I didn't know any of this at the time, however. I passed out again or went to sleep soon after being picked up.

I don't remember anything else until waking up next morning in the Royal Naval Hospital at Great Yarmouth. One of Lt Moody's crew was with me but I didn't know his name and didn't get it later. We were in a large ward with probably ten Royal Navy seamen.

The Royal Navy served the two of us a breakfast of bacon and eggs, an extremely rare commodity in wartime England. I tried to eat but had swallowed so much seawater that even the mildly salted bacon was unpleasant. The Royal Navy seamen couldn't help staring at our feast. In a moment of clarity I asked the seaman next to me if he could finish my breakfast. He and a couple of others gratefully accepted. I remember vividly to this day that it was almost like a feeding frenzy. It had been a long time since an enlisted Englishman had that kind of food.

Somewhere along here I began to realize that while the US was *at* war, England was *in* the war. A subtle, but very real difference!

A B-17 was sent to take us back to the 390th from a very short grass strip. It had been neutered (all armaments removed) and may have been somewhat squirrelly to fly. In any event, the pilot landed a bit long and the tail lifted off the ground as he braked to stop. I remember thinking, "Dammit, we're going to be killed by an incompetent pilot who was supposed to be on our side!"

We were given two weeks R&R at Berkley House, a beautiful English country estate (castle) but I couldn't enjoy all of the facilities because my chipped elbow was still quite sore. I did thoroughly enjoy being able to study the exquisite workmanship of the medieval suits of armour standing in the hallways. We were told that Berkley House had been set up to receive the British Government if a German invasion were successful.

After returning to the USA I wrote a descriptive letter to Don Downey's parents but without their address I was unable to get it delivered and as a nineteen-year-old I wasn't very innovative in finding ways "around the system". In 1992 we visited Jackson, MS where Don had lived, and I tried unsuccessfully to locate any family that might be interested.

No attempt was made to communicate any of this to the family of the British crew members killed on the air-sea rescue boat. As with Don, it's probably academic now.

*Fortress of 390th Bomb Group 8th Air Force taking off for a mission over Europe late 1943 or early 1944 [**courtesy of E.A. Munday**]*

A B-17 Flying Fortress of 390th Bomber Group on the hard standing at Framlingham.

Lt.E. Moody (bottom centre) and the crew of B-17 G, No 297830 'E' Easy.
[390th Bomb Group Assoc USAF]

14. An American Patrol – 1944-1945

American involvement in air sea rescue was very limited and slow. The 8th and 9th USAAF relied totally on the Royal Air Force and Royal Navy rescue services, both of which they held in high esteem. But as in all things the Americans learned quickly and had one squadron – the 5th Emergency Rescue Service – up and running in January 1945.

Thanks to the experiences gained in wartime, in the post-war years the US had an air-sea rescue service with rescue boats, aircraft, amphibians and coastguards which was second to none.

One flight of the 5th ERS came into being in May 1944 at Boxted in Essex. They were equipped with war-weary P-47 Thunderbolts with under wing containers containing British 'M'-type dinghies and racks with smoke marker bombs. In January 1945 the 5th re-located to Halesworth in Suffolk. With additional types of aircraft – PBY 5a Catalinas and B-17 bombers with under-slung lifeboats.

Until this time the Americans had no seaplanes or amphibians operating a rescue service and relied solely on their P-47s working with the British ASR services.

On 30th March 1945 the American Air-Sea Rescue Squadron suffered its first losses in a major multiple rescue off the Dutch Frisian Islands. A Catalina flying boat (PBY-5A in the US Navy but OA-10s in the Army Air Force) flown by Lt Hicks went to the aid of a B24 Liberator Bomber of the 491st Bomb Group (based at North Pickenham) which had been damaged by flak and was going to ditch. The Catalina sighted the bomber but on ditching the B-24 broke in two. Despite the heavy seas the Catalina landed and picked up two survivors but the flying-boat was taking on water and was unable to take-off. Lt Hicks sent a Mayday signal to another Catalina and a nearby rescue launch. It was the rescue launch that made the pick-up and rescued Lt Hicks and his crew, together with the two B-24 survivors. The Catalina consequently sank.

Meanwhile a P-51 Mustang of 357th FG (from Yoxford, Suffolk) piloted by Lt D. Meyers was damaged by enemy fighters over Hamburg, Northern Germany. He turned for home but had to bale out five miles north of the Frisian Island of Schiermonkoog. A PBY 5a Catalina (callsign Teamwork

75) from the 5th ERS Halesworth was called to his rescue. The seas were running high with six-foot waves when the pilot was spotted. The Catalina pilot, Capt Laponas, attempted a landing but as he did so waves fractured an oil pipe to one of the engines and he was unable to manoeuvre to make the pick up. His troubles were only just beginning... He was spotted on the surface by a Messerschmitt Me 262 from IJG7 (Lubeck), piloted by Lt Weihs, who then made two passes over the Catalina, raking it with cannon fire. The tail was shot off, as was the port wing float.

Capt Laponas gave the order to abandon the aircraft and take to the dinghies. This was witnessed by three Mustangs of 357th FG, who had covered their comrades decent into the sea. A Vickers Warwick from 280 Squadron ASR (Beccles) was called to drop an airborne life-boat. The drop was satisfactory, but it was swept away in the high seas.

A third Catalina (Teamwork 70) from No.5 ERS was despatched and attempted a landing, but came under intense gunfire from the shore batteries on the enemy-held coast and the rescue was aborted. A B-17 with a Lindholme lifeboat, piloted by Lt Newark, then took off from Halesworth, Suffolk and made a successful drop (the first operational drop of an airborne lifeboat by the Americans). This time the Catalina crew managed to get aboard. The Mustang pilot, Lt Mayers, was swept onto the island of Schiermonkoog and captured by the Germans. Two Royal Naval rescue boats were sent by HMS *Midge* (Great Yarmouth) but the sea conditions were so bad they had to return to port.

The late Patrick Troughton (later to become an actor and the second *Doctor Who*) was, at the time, senior officer of the RNLs.

This is his story of the operation:

"I was sent out as Senior Officer of the unit of "Z" Boats (Naval Rescue Craft) in my own boat (RML 514) along with RML 498. We were told that a Vickers Warwick would rendezvous with us and drop flares to guide us to the American airmen in their lifeboat. About midnight I sighted a flare and succeeded in making contact with the Warwick, which was coming in on the automatic transmitter in the lifeboat. By this time we were well into the Helgoland Bight. We were told where the lifeboat was, but because of the high seas and the darkness we couldn't find it. I therefore decided to cut the engines and drift with the wind and tide until daybreak.

At first light (April 4th) we sighted the lifeboat about a quarter of a mile on our beam. I signalled RML 498 which went in and made the pick-up. Being too rough to take the lifeboat in tow, we (RMLs 498 and 514) opened fire and sank her. We returned to Great Yarmouth in the early hours of 5th April.

The rescue operation had lasted seven days and had used all the resources of the air-sea rescue services – Royal Navy, Royal Air Force and the American Emergency Rescue Services. The rescue aircraft, both RAF and USAAF, had remained overhead on both April 3rd and 4th, dropping flares and remaining in contact – and all this within 30 miles of the enemy coast.

A generous tribute was paid by the Officer Commanding 5th Emergency Rescue Squadron Halesworth to the Commanding Officers of both RML 514 and RML 498:

"On behalf of my crews and myself, I would like to take this opportunity to express our deepest admiration to the Officers and Men who saved their lives of the Catalina Crew in the Heligoland Bight on 4th April 1945.

Due to the adverse weather conditions and the sea condition the courage and determination displayed by both Rescue Launches and Rescue Aircraft will long be remembered. We thank each and every one of those Officers and Men in one of the most daring rescues on record.

Signed by:

Lt J. Laponas   Lt T.J. Langan   Lt C.J. Buffington
Sgt W. Dotson Sgt J. McMullen Sgt D. Hochstatter

A Catalina flying-foat of the 5th Emergency Rescue Service (ERS) at Halesworth, Suffolk. These were known as PBY 5A in the US Navy or OA-10 in the US Army Air Force.

RML 514 (Patrick Troughton) in foreground with an Airborne Lifeboat alongside RML 517
or 519, in the background is HSL 2707 (Hants & Dorset) 68 ft.
[RAF Museum Cardington]

15. The Scoby Sands Incident –January 1945

January 1945 started with a bang. Although the war was in its closing months and the German land forces were being pushed back, the Kriegsmarine (German Navy) were still a force to be reckoned with, especially in the southern sector of the North Sea. Having been deprived of the Northern French and Belgian ports (Ostend had fallen to the Allies on September 9th 1944) they could still muster some 50 E-Boats and some 24 *Seehund* (2-man midget submarines) and *Biber* (1-man submarines) operating out of the Dutch ports of Den Helder, Rotterdam and Ijmuiden. On the night of 13/14th January 1945 the E-Boats, together with the midget submarines, carried out one of their biggest operations since 1943. Four Royal Navy Destroyers were engaged and four sizable merchant ships sunk. Again on 16th and 23rd January, E-Boats ventured right up the Thames estuary.

It was against this background that one of the most bizarre rescues took place off Great Yarmouth. On the night of 24th January, ML 153 attacked a *Seehund* two-man midget submarine (No.5303) to the south of the Scoby sandbank. The two-man crew managed to escape, and with the aid of an inflatable life-raft, drifted onto the north end of the Scoby Elbow. This was on the 27th January.

Finding all chances of escape cut off, they fired distress flares. These were seen by the Trinity House vessel *Beacon* and also Air-Sea Rescue launch HSL 2507, which was on passage from Grimsby to Ramsgate. The ASR launch was of shallow draught and managed to get close enough to allow the Germans to get aboard. They were delivered to 24 ASRU at Gorleston and placed in the custody of the Army. They turned out to be the first captives from an enemy midget submarine and the intelligence services were particularly interested in the crew's belongings, as they were thought to be an indication of how the Royal Navy's blockade of German held ports was progressing.

This must have been a significant rescue because it was even mentioned on Berlin radio by "Lord Haw-Haw". Unfortunately the HSL crew missed their moment of glory as they were celebrating at the local hostelry. Later intelligence reveals that U-5303 was part of a group of ten midget submarines attacking shipping north of the English Channel. Unfortunately U-

5303 suffered a compass failure and set off towards Ijmuiden. The submarine was detected North of Lowestoft by ML 153 and attacked. She had laid on the bottom for some time, but the tides dragged her onto the Scoby sandbank, where she stuck fast.

Two-man 'Seehund' midget submarines, January 1945.

16. A Job Well Done

With the cessation of hostilities in Europe in May 1945, the full story of what had been achieved by 24 ASRU began to emerge. From its humble beginnings in 1940 when it was just a satellite station to RAF Felixstowe, with the occasional launch mooring up near the wooden huts at Baker Street it had become, by 1944, a base with its own Commanding Officer and a rescue system that had its own plotting room (Shadingfield Lodge[3]) on the Marine Parade at Great Yarmouth, and operated in conjunction with the Royal Navy, the Royal Air Force Air Sea Rescue Squadrons and the American Air Force with their own Rescue Services.

At its height the base operated between 16 and 20 high speed launches and could call on the assistance of four Royal Navy rescue craft to cover the East Anglian coastline from Kings Lynn in the north to the Thames Estuary in the south – probably the busiest sector of airspace anywhere in the world during this period (as one who witnessed it from the ground, I can state that both night and day the sky was never still.)

It is not surprising therefore, that some 700 lives were saved by Royal Air Force Air-Sea Rescue units operating from the East Coast; this figure represents 10% of all aircrew lives saves by the RAF Rescue Service. And Gorleston was both the busiest and the most successful ASR base in the United Kingdom.

The climax came on 9th of March 1944, when no fewer than four rescues took place during a space of a few hours. These were carried out by HSLs 158 and 2697 and RMLs 514 and 498; between them they rescued 28 American aircrew from the North Sea.

From the beginning of 1943 to the end of hostilities, 538 personnel were saved from the sea. But this great record was not achieved without loss. One boat captured, its wireless operator was killed and the remainder of the crew spending the rest of the war interned in prisoner of war camps; another launch shot up by enemy aircraft and sunk with the loss of both crew and their rescued comrades; and another launch shot up and sunk by

---

[3] Shadingfield Lodge had been a Royal Navy centre since the formation of the RN base units HMS *Midge* and *Miranda* along the River Yare.

'friendly fire' through mistaken identity, with the consequent loss of almost all her crew.

A satellite to Gorleston was set up at Lowestoft in the summer of 1943, still under the designation of 24 ASRU and operated the same launches, many of which travelled to Lowestoft by the inland route – under the Haven Bridge across Breydon Water to the village of Reedham, and then down the Haddiscoe Cut (the Ship Inn at Haddiscoe Bridge was a favourite 'halfway house' and I am told that the landlord served ales to the crew of both MTBs and HSLs from 7am until midnight, well outside the regular hours, if the boats were moored there for the night).

There remains little or else to be said. The need for the wartime base had passed. The job had been done and done well, and there were many grateful mothers, wives and sweethearts who had every reason to be thankful to the officers, NCOs and men of 24 ASRU for saving the lives of their loved-ones.

17. Peacetime – But Tasks Continue

By the end of 1945 there was a rush to return to civilian life after six years of war. The Cliff Hotel reverted to its peacetime role of catering for the holiday trade. The base in Baker Street and the wooden barracks remained open and operational, although the command of the base, once again came under the umbrella of RAF Felixstowe, just as it had been in 1940. The last of the whalebacks were pensioned off but the Hants & Dorset's soldiered on well into the 1960s. The launches lost all of their trappings of war, the gun turrets and matt grey paint; instead all the upper works were painted a pale blue-grey with white tops.

The rescue launches carried out exercises and simulated rescues with the newfangled flying machines known as *helicopters*, the first of these being the Sikorsky S-51 Dragonfly, followed by the Bristol Sycamore and the later the Sikorsky S-55 Whirlwind. These were based with 202 squadron at RAF Coltishall. A large helicopter pad was laid out behind the barracks at Baker Street so that the launches and helicopters could work with one another and the helicopters were regular visitors to the base.

Although hostilities had ceased, the East Anglian coastline was still a very busy area of air space. The run-down of the wartime airfields had not yet begun and the law of averages still said that accidents had to happen.

On 14th June 1950 a B-29 Super Fortress ditched 30 miles northeast of Cromer. It is not known which bomb group the B-29 came from, but the current research shows that B-29s were based at Bassingbourne (Cambridgeshire) and Mildenhall and Lakenheath in Norfolk. Whilst on gunnery training, all groups operated out of Sculthorpe in Norfolk (this applied also to B-29 squadrons based in Europe). This particular B-29 was on gunnery exercises in the North Sea when part of a gun turret exploded and pierced the starboard outer engine, causing a fire. The pilot went into a standard procedure and dived to put out the fire, but this made matters worse so he decided to ditch.

The first vessel on the scene was a Norwegian coaster, which picked up three survivors in a dinghy. They were transferred to HSL 2259 and brought into Great Yarmouth. A fourth survivor was brought in by a Royal Navy gunboat. There were no other survivors.

On 20th May 1952 two Meteor night fighters from 141 Squadron at RAF Coltishall collided near the Cross-Sands lightship. One of the aircraft managed to return to base but the pilot and navigator of the other aircraft ejected. The pilot got into his dinghy, but there was no sign of the naviga-tor.[4] Both an air-sea rescue launch from No.24 ASRU at Gorleston and the Caister Lifeboat were launched. An American air-sea rescue Grumman Albatross Amphibian from Manston in Kent was also involved. It was the Albatross that sighted the pilot and landed in heavy seas to make the pick-up but unfortunately the aircraft was damaged and unable to take off again. The rescue launch, together with two lifeboats, escorted the am-phibian back to Great Yarmouth harbour, where the Albatross "waddled up" on Spending Beach to discharge the pilot to a waiting ambulance.

After two days on Spending Beach being tended by American engineers from nearby Shepard's Grove airfield, the Albatross taxied out of Yarmouth harbour into the roads, took off and headed back to base.

Another rescue occurred in 1963, when an F-100 Super-Sabre from USAF Lakenheath was on exercise in the North Sea (low-level bombing practice on Scoby sandbank) when it experienced engine problems. Knowing that a return to base was out of the question the pilot put out a 'mayday', pointed the aircraft out to sea, and ejected. An RAF launch on detachment at Gorleston was despatched to pick him up. Unfortunately, the aircraft did a U-turn back towards the coast, and crashed into the mud on Darby's Hard on the Gorleston riverbank, narrowly missing the Birds-Eye factory.

The aircraft buried itself into the mud, which reduced the damage caused, although there were a few broken windows in Gorleston High Street and three fishing boats on Darby's Hard were burned out, but fortunately there were no causalities.

Other duties undertaken by the unit prior to its closure were by Rescue Target Towing Launches (RTTLs), which towed "splash targets" some 600 yards astern for bombing and cannon practice by aircraft.

In the early part of 1959 all Marine Craft Units in the United Kingdom established only for the primary task of search and rescue were closed and the role was taken over by helicopters. The closures included 1103 MCU at RAF Felixstowe, of which the Gorleston base was a detachment. The two buildings at Baker Street were placed on care and maintenance for a brief period and eventually taken over by the Royal Observer Corps and the Air

---

[4] Whilst researching this story, the author found that the missing navigator was the son of one of the foremost doctors in Yarmouth, a Dr Adlington.

Training Corps. Due to an oversight by the MOD (Air) the lease was not renewed and in 1962 the base was reduced to rubble. However, the Baker Street quayside had not seen the last of RAF Marine craft...

1104 MCU RAF Bridlington had been closed as a range safety base following the introduction of marine VHF radio into general use by fishing craft, merchant ships and many private craft. This allowed the range control tower at RAF Cowden to broadcast range use times and warn off any vessels intruding into the danger areas, formally the task of the patrolling Range Safety Launches.

In the summer of 1959 1104 MCU was re-opened and with the established primary task of providing wet winching training facilities for the search and rescue (SAR) helicopter flights based at RAF Leconfield plus RAF Acklington (later RAF Boulmer) and RAF Leuchars in Scotland, to the north and RAF Coltishall and later RAF Manston to the south. For the vessels of 1104 MCU search and rescue was to be a secondary task only.

Aircrew from RAF flying stations in the eastern UK were also to take part in the above training as live "survivors", following immersion in the sea, dinghy drill and simulated parachute dragging.

For this role a WW2-era 60ft GS Pinnace and an SD Pinnace were established at 1104 MCU and a programme developed which involved the monthly detachment of one craft to the northern ports of Blyth or Amble and thence to Tayport or Dundee and other craft southwards to Gorleston and later Ramsgate. Each crew was away on tasks for some ten to fourteen days, each helicopter flight normally requiring a minimum of three days of exercises.

The first two vessels were eventually replaced by newer 63ft Pinnaces, which continued to use the Baker Street moorings monthly, year after year until 1976, when in turn they were replaced by two steel-hulled Mk.III RTTLs (over the years the task of 1104 MCU had been expanded to include target-towing for RAF aircraft on the sea range in the Smith's Knoll area).

In 1986 the RAF Marine Branch closed and its operational requirements were taken over by civilian contractors James Fisher & Co of Barrow in Furness, who won the first contract. They opened an office at George Prior Engineering Ltd's shipyard in Great Yarmouth and stationed two Mk III RTTLs on the nearby quayside. These craft continued to wear RAF roundels on each bow but flew the Government auxiliary vessel blue ensign and were crewed by civilians, some of whom were newly-discharged RAF mariners. The contract eventually changed hands but the craft continued to operate out of the port.

In late 2003 the Mk IIIs, now some 25 or more years old, were retired and replaced by a modern, all-aluminium vessel of similar length. The new craft, *Smit Yare*, now owned and managed by one of the Smit Group Companies, continues to sail from the Town Hall quay area. Its specifications are:

Designers & Builders	FBM Babcock Marine Ltd
Place of Build	CEBU Philippines
Length	28.95 metres
Beam	6.6 metres
Weight	full load 58 tonnes approx
Engines	2 x Cummins KTA 19MA (Marine Engines) 700 HP @ 2100 RPM
	1 x Loiter Cummins 350HP @ 2500RPM Operating through Water Jet
	2 x Cummins Generators
Speed	22.5 Knots, service speed 15 knots
Fuel Capacity	6.32 Tons in 2 Main Tanks plus 1 daily tank
Range	650 nautical miles @ 15 knots
Mono Hull (Low maintenance Marine Grade Aluminium) Twin Mechanical Link Rudders 3 Bladed Propellers ZF Gearboxes	
Heating	2 warm/cool Air Blowers
Deck fitted	Offer 2600/16 Hydraulic Crane
Upper Deck	Wheelhouse
Middle Deck	Captain/Engineer cabins, shower and toilet
Lower Deck	Galley/Washroom/4 Crew Cabins/Mess Room
Area of Operation	Southern North Sea (Yorkshire to Kent) Based at Great Yarmouth
Tasking	Dinghy Drill, Target Towing, Winching for Helicopters
Capacity to carry up to 12 aircrew, who have their own two showers	

Thus for 64 years 1940–2004 the ports of Great Yarmouth and Gorleston have created a proud record of hosting Royal Air Force Air Sea Rescue Service boats, Royal Air Force Marine Branch vessels during the postwar years until 1986 and then for 17 years acting as a base for civilian-crewed ex-RAF vessels and is currently home port for the latest class of Aircraft Support Craft, the *Smit Yare* – a very honourable history and achievement and a significant part of the port's maritime heritage.

Hopefully in 2005 a memorial will be erected on Brush Quay at Gorleston to celebrate and record the long-standing connection between RAF mariners and the town.

Baker Street during 1944. Seven HSLs form a flotilla. These would be sent to rendezvous positions on the flight paths of bombers and fighters returning from missions over Europe. On the opposite bank are Royal Navy Minesweepers.

HMAFV[5] 4001 "Sunderland"
This type of steel-hulled craft replaced HSLs in the 1970s.

---

[5] Her Majesty's Royal Air Force Vessel – a title allowed on all RAF craft over 60ft.

Painting which hangs in the entrance hall of the Cliff Hotel, commemorating the occupation of the hotel by Launch crews from 1941 until 1945.

*On the left, an American aircrew rescued from a B-29, on board a Royal Navy Gun Boat at Great Yarmouth [**L. Gould**].*

Grumman Albatross being towed into Great Yarmouth Harbour.
[The Williment Collection]

The injured pilot is removed onto a stretcher. [L. Gould].

Albatross being repaired at Spending Beach. [L. Gould]

1958 or 9– RAF Pinnace 77– a GP Pinnace equipped for Air Sea Rescue. Her aft gun turret has been removed. Entering Gt Yarmouth Harbour, the North pier in the background. **[R. Allard]**

RAF Pinnace 1386 – an updated version of the GP Pinnace and noticeably different from the version in the previous photograph. Seen entering Great Yarmouth Harbour. In the background is the Oil Exploration vessel Glomar IV **[R. Allard]**

*Westland helicopters eventually replaced the RAF Rescue launches. Seen here demonstrating a rescue off Gt. Yarmouth. [**The Westland Company**]*

*GP Pinnace 1397 accompanied by a Westland Whirlwind helicopter in a rescue demonstration off the harbour mouth at Great Yarmouth. [**R. Allard**]*

HSL 2579 – a "Hants & Dorset" launch built in 1942 – converted in 1950 (gun turrets removed). Seen here leaving Gt Yarmouth en route to Felixstowe. **[G. Joell]**

HSL 2559 returning from a patrol during 1950s. Post-war she was classed as an RTTL (Rescue and Target-Towing Launch). These would tow target well astern for fighter aircraft to use for air-to-surface target practice. **[G. Joell]**

GP Pinnace 1383 moored up in the Yare opposite Baker Street in the late 50s. The large air intake by the wheelhouse provided fresh to the engine room. **[G. Joell]**

GP Pinnace 1383 entering Gt Yarmouth Harbour 1950s **[G. Joell]**

*GP Pinnace 1387 from 1104 MCU Bridlington in harbour entrance 1964
Crew: Flt Lt Armstrong (Skipper) Sgt Sammy Johnstone (Cox'n) Cpl Doran (Fitter)
SAC Gray (W/Op) and the deckhands were SAC Dave Theobald,
SAC Eric Jackson and SAC Jock Smith.* **[D. Smith]**

*GP Pinnace 1392 from Bridlington 1970 – a Mk 2 turbocharged boat – the last wooden boat ever built for the RAF. [**D. Smith**]*

*RTTL (Hants & Dorset) 2559. Entering harbour 1954 on detachment from 1107 MCU Felixstowe. [**D. Smith**]*

HMAFV RTTL Mk 3 "STIRLING" running in c1980. **[D. Smith]**

"Smit Yare" in Harwich Harbour awaiting aircrew trainees. **[S. Mckay]**

18. In Conclusion

On 12th November 1988 there was a grand reunion of some 35 former personnel of No.24 ASRU Gorleston, along with their wives, at the Cliff Hotel. For one particular member, who had not been back since 1942, the sight of the glass chandeliers and burgundy and gold flock wallpaper seemed far removed from those days of austerity when sombre green and cream paint with thick brown linoleum on the floors was the decor. A superb meal was followed by tributes to the Air-Sea Rescue crews by the Mayor of Great Yarmouth. Many acquaintances were made and many a comradeship re-kindled. There was, of course, much "lamp swinging" and, above all, remembrance of those who fell in combat or departed in the years since. The night went well and many a heavy head was felt the following morning!

On the Sunday morning, it being Remembrance Sunday, the veterans went aboard the Air-Sea Tender *Lancaster*, together with the Reverend David Moyse of St Andrew's Church, Gorleston, who conducted a service of remembrance offshore for those members of the Air-Sea Rescue Service who had laid down their lives in the service of their country. At the end of the service, wreaths were laid at sea for all who perished. It was indeed a fitting tribute to the service in general and in particular No.24 ASRU, whose fine record was truly worthy of the ASR motto:

"THE SEA SHALL NOT HAVE THEM"

Brothers

I know that I'm slow, the old fellow replied,
And I'm often a crushing old bore,
But I once helped to salvage our nation's pride,
Brought low on an enemy shore.

Of course there were thousands of others
Who had rallied to rescue their kin,
For in those days it seemed we were brothers,
And as brothers we would win.

And later I sailed with a mighty host,
With the greatest armada of all,
And I shared in the fear as the moment drew near,
To assault that impregnable wall.
But of course there were thousands of others,
Who'd returned to regain what we'd lost,
So we shared in our triumph like brothers.

And now that the fighting has ended,
And the things that we fought for are won,
We are surely entitled to let our down our hair,
And abandon ourselves to some fun.

But of course there were thousands of others,
Whose lives are forever impaired,
Lets spare them a thought, they're our brothers,
Lets remind them at least that we cared.

Group Captain L.R. Flower, MBE, MM

*Veteran RAF Mariners who served at No24 ASRU during WW2 aboard RTTL **Lancaster**
to lay wreaths at sea in memory of their colleagues who have no known graves apart from
the North Sea. [**D. Thurston**]*

*RTTL.4006 Lancaster moving off from her moorings at Great Yarmouth to lay wreaths off
Gorleston where a service of remembrance was held. [**D.Thurston**]*

RAF Launches which served at Gorleston or Lowestoft

HSL 108	Captured off Holland on 1st July 1941
	W/Op Killed. Rest of crew captured.
HSL 2551	Lost due to enemy action on 29th June 1944
	3 crewmen and 2 Americans killed, 7 crewmen injured.
	Skipper died of hypothermia.
HSL 2706	Lost due to USAAF action on 3rd March 1944.
	Out of 13 crew only 2 survived; one lost an arm and a leg.

Gorleston			Lowestoft		
HSLs	HSLs	LRRCs	HSLs	HSLs	LRRCs
116	2550	003	2560	2691	014
124	2551	004	2594	2696	004
125	2555	012	2677	2697	
130	2556	014	2679		
132	2560				
144	2594				
158	2631				
159	2677				
168	2679				
169	2691				
170	2694				
171	2697				
180	2707				
184					
185					

Also published by Woodfield

In the Nick of Time by Nick Berryman

In this entertaining memoir the author recalls his experiences as a RAF air/sea rescue pilot during World War II. Based at Warmwell on the South Coast he flew the Spitfire and Walrus over the English Channel in search of stranded RAF aircrews whose aircraft had been shot down or forced to ditch. He has a many remarkable stories to tell.

Swinging the Lamp by Ted Bedwell

In an enjoyable memoir the author recalls a wealth of incidents from his lengthy career as a RAF HSL and Pinnace Coxswain involving a wide variety of situations that could only occur at sea, many of which are very funny indeed. Guaranteed to amuse anyone with a military or nautical background.

Very Unable Seaman by Richard Barr

The author recalls his experiences as an inept junior seaman serving aboard HMS *Rampart* in the late 1950s. One of the Navy's less glamorous vessels, *Rampart*, a former World War II LCT (Landing Craft Tank L4037), was home to a small but happy crew of colourful nautical characters, whose antics at sea and ashore are fondly remembered in an entertaining and amusing account that will appeal to anyone with nautical experience.

All the above plus many more books on a wide variety of subjects available from the Woodfield Publishing website
www.woodfieldpublishing.co.uk
telephone orders 01243 821234